RIDE OR DIE

365 Day Bible Plan

Mantour Ministries

Published by 4One Ministries, Inc. Visit www.mantourministries.com for more information on bulk discounts and special promotions, or e-mail your questions to info@4oneministries.org.

Design: James J. Holden

Subject Headings:
1. Christian life 2. Men's Ministry 3. Spiritual Growth

ISBN 978-1-7378821-2-1

Printed in the United States of America

-WEEK ONE-

BY JAMIE HOLDEN

It was a typical day, and I was looking for some tunes to listen to while I went about my routine. I said, *"Alexa, play something by Toby Mac."*

Next thing you know, the song *"Ignition"* is blaring through my house.

Even though I've heard this song a million times before, today, as I listened, the line about *"riding or dying"* for Christ jumped out of my Alexa device and into my ears.

I'd had heard this phrase before and never given it much thought, but that day it really stood out to me. So I decided to do a little research.

According to Dictionary.com, a *"ride or die"* is *"a colloquial expression of extreme loyalty to someone or something."*[1]

The Urban Dictionary defines it as *"when you are willing to do anything for someone you love or someone you really appreciate in your life. You ride or die for the person who stood by you in any problem and vice versa."*[2]

So basically, to *"ride or die"* means you will do anything for the person you love. There is nothing they could ask of you that you would not be willing to do. It means you will go to the ends of the earth for them, take risks for them, and stand by them no matter the cost. You will ride with them even if it ends up killing you. It's a statement of extreme loyalty and devotion to someone else.

As I read this, I remembered a passage of scripture from Matthew 16:24-26:

> *Then Jesus said to his disciples, "Whoever wants to be my*
> *disciple must deny themselves and take up their cross and*
> *follow me. For whoever wants to save their life will lose it,*
> *but whoever loses their life for me will find it. What good*
> *will it be for someone to gain the whole world, yet forfeit*
> *their soul? Or what can anyone give in exchange for their*
> *soul?" (NIV)*

To spiritually ride or die means we have to pick up our cross for Jesus.

No matter where you are or what you are facing, I believe God has a challenge for you to take in your life. He wants to ask you, *"Will you ride or die with Me?"*

Will you ride or die with Him if He takes your perfect life and turns it upside down?

How about if what He asks goes against the cultural norms? What if He asks to stand for something the Twitter mob won't like?

What if He asks you to go in a completely different direction in your career or calling?

Will you commit to ride or die if He shakes your comfort zone?

What about if He asks you to take a ginormous leap of faith for Him?

Are you still willing to ride or die?

I believe that one of the key factors in being a ride or die man of God is being a man who is dedicated to God's Word. That's why I am so passionate about our daily Bible reading plan designed especially for men.

It is not a *"through the Bible in a year"* plan. Instead, we have chosen to weed through some of the *"begets"* and places where they count sheep and bowls and focus on designing a few chapters for you to read each day.

There are two chapters in the Bible for you to read on Monday-Saturday and a Psalm or Proverb. (I believe there is so much wisdom in these two books they deserve special attention!) Each day also has a memory verse. If you choose to read through this verse two to three times throughout your day, you will have memorized or at least be very familiar with the books of James, 1 and 2 Peter and Philippians by the end of the year.

On Sundays, we've invited our Mantour speakers to join me and write about a real-life man who decided to ride or die with Christ. Some of their stories are found in the Bible, others are historical, and some are men we've encountered in our own lives. These men were real guys, just like you or me. They had strengths as well as a whole lot of weaknesses and flaws. Each one of them had to make hard choices to ride or die with God. I hope their stories inspire you to make the choices they made, that no matter what they encountered, what trials they faced, or whatever God required of them, they would ride or die with Him!

To reach as many men as possible, we're making this year's Bible Reading Plan available in digital or paperback. Whether you receive an email each day for free, or you choose a written copy, whether you work through it on your own or with a group of men, it is my prayer that this resource will inspire you to read God's Word every day, make it a part of your routine, and develop a deep love for it. As you grow in God's Word, I pray you, too, will accept the challenge to be a ride or die man of God.

Are you ready to go? Let's start our journey together as we learn to ride or die with God!

-Jamie Holden, Founder, Mantour Ministries

Monday

John 1-3 ☐   Psalm 1-2 ☐

Memory Verse*: Consider it pure joy, my brothers and sisters, whenever you face trials of many kinds, because you know that the testing of your faith produces perseverance.* (James 1:2-3, NIV)

Tuesday

John 4-6 ☐   Proverbs 1:1-19 ☐

Memory Verse: *Let perseverance finish its work so that you may be mature and complete, not lacking anything.* (James 1:4, NIV)

Wednesday

John 7-8, ☐   Psalm 3 ☐

Memory Verse: *If any of you lacks wisdom, you should ask God, who gives generously to all without finding fault, and it will be given to you.* (James 1:5, NIV)

Thursday

John 9-10 ☐   Proverbs 1:20-33 ☐

Memory Verse: *But when you ask, you must believe and not doubt, because the one who doubts is like a wave of the sea, blown and tossed by the wind.* (James 1:6, NIV)

Friday

John 11-12 ☐   Psalm 4 ☐

Memory Verse: *That person should not expect to receive anything from the Lord. Such a person is double-minded and unstable in all they do.* (James 1:7-8, NIV)

Saturday

John 13-14 ☐   Psalm 5 ☐

Memory Verse: *Believers in humble circumstances ought to take pride in their high position.* (James 1:9, NIV)

THOUGHTS AND

REFLECTIONS

-WEEK TWO-

JAN OPPERMAN: THE RACING HIPPIE
BY JIM PENTZ

The year was 1969. It was the summer between my junior and senior years of high school. I spent my summer Saturday nights at the Selinsgrove Speedway, a very fast half-mile clay race track in central Pennsylvania – the heart of the northeast auto racing community.

A couple of high school buddies and I worked in the pits for a local sprint car driver. We were gaining experience and saving money with the dream of buying our own car and going racing. But God had other plans.

Proverbs 16:9 says, "In his heart, a man plans his course, but the Lord determines his steps." (NIV)

Because the racing was so good in central Pennsylvania, drivers came from around the country to compete. That is how I met *"The Racing Hippie,"* Jan Opperman. On his first night at the track, Jan competed wheel-to-wheel with one of the best drivers in the track's history. I was impressed with his ability to drive a race car, but I also was intrigued that he was a long-haired, free-spirited *"hippie."* Remember, it was 1969, and I was an impressionable seventeen-year-old. Fast cars and a free spirit were what made my world go round.

I was somewhere between impressed and intrigued when God began to work in my life. He was working in Jan's life as well. Jan made a solid commitment to the Lord Jesus Christ, and the Racing Hippie became the Racing Evangelist. After every win, he would give glory to God. He interacted with competitors and fans with genuine grace. He modeled what it meant to be outstanding in your profession while being humble in your confession. As a seventeen-year-old racing enthusiast, I wanted to be just like Jan.

During that same time, I made my personal confession of faith in the Lordship of Jesus Christ. Now not only was I impressed and intrigued by Jan Opperman, but his changed life also inspired me, his commitment to Jesus Christ, and his desire to help others find Christ as well.

Jan went on to race in the Indianapolis 500, *"The Greatest Spectacle in Racing,"* along with many other major races at premier venues. Right up until his death, Jan Opperman was a *"Ride or Die Man of God."* He was using his name recognition and his winnings to build a ranch in western Montana to help troubled youth come out of the drug culture and find real life in Jesus Christ.

In Luke 12:48, Jesus tells us, ***"From everyone who has been given much, much will be demanded; and from the one who has been entrusted with much, much more will be asked."*** (NIV) Jan was given much talent and much recognition; he also gave back to those who were less fortunate than himself. Except for the grace of God, he could have been one of those *"troubled youth."* Because of the grace of God, he was there to help.

I often wonder how different my life might have been had I not had the privilege of meeting Jan Opperman at the very time that he met the Lord. God's timing is amazing, and God certainly used him to change me.

Regardless of how you are known to the world, what you are good at, or what you are known by, always be a *"Ride or Die Man of God."* Always be willing to give your all for the One Who gave His all for you.

For your consideration:

Who has God brought into your life at just the right time to help you change for the good?

What has God entrusted to you? How are you using that for the benefit of others?

Today's Scripture: From everyone who has been given much, much will be demanded; and from the one who has been entrusted with much, much more will be asked. (Luke 12:48)

-Pastor Jim Pentz, Lead Pastor, New Covenant Assembly, Montgomery, PA Presbyter, North Central Section of the PennDel Ministry Network

Monday

John 15-16 ☐   Psalm 6 ☐

Memory Verse: *But the rich should take pride in their humiliation— since they will pass away like a wild flower.* (James 1:10, NIV)

Tuesday

John 17-18 ☐   Proverbs 2:1-11 ☐

Memory Verse: *For the sun rises with scorching heat and withers the plant; its blossom falls and its beauty is destroyed. In the same way, the rich will fade away even while they go about their business.* (James 1:11, NIV)

Wednesday

John 19-20 ☐   Psalm 7 ☐

Memory Verse: *Blessed is the one who perseveres under trial because, having stood the test, that person will receive the crown of life that the Lord has promised to those who love him.* (James 1:12, NIV)

Thursday

John 21 ☐   Proverbs 2:12-22 ☐

Memory Verse: *When tempted, no one should say, "God is tempting me."*
For God cannot be tempted by evil, nor does he tempt anyone; (James
1:13, NIV)

Friday

Joshua 1-2 ☐   Psalm 8 ☐

Memory Verse: *But each person is tempted when they are dragged away*
by their own evil desire and enticed. (James 1:14, NIV)

Saturday

Joshua 3-4 ☐   Psalm 9 ☐

Memory Verse: *Then, after desire has conceived, it gives birth to sin; and*
sin, when it is full-grown, gives birth to death. (James 1:15, NIV)

-WEEK THREE-

ANANIAS
BY JAMIE HOLDEN

Y*ou've got to be kidding me?"*

"There's no way God would want me to do that! I must not be hearing right!"

"Seriously, God, You want me to do what?"

All of these thoughts and more must have been racing through Ananias' mind when God told him to go and pray for Saul of Tarsus.

After all, Ananias was just a regular guy trying to live for God and do the right thing.

Saul was not regular at all. He was quite powerful. More importantly, he passionately hated Christians and used his power to persecute them. He hunted them down to put them in prison and kill them. Now God was asking Ananias to visit him?

Ananais' first response was: No way, not happening, too dangerous. Followed by, *"God, do You know who he is and what he does?"*

Then God replied, *"I know...but I've called him to be my servant... now you go."*

So Ananias went.

But we mustn't read over this too lightly. We need to understand that Ananais' choice to see Saul was a ride or die moment. Every part of Ananais' intellect told him there was a very good chance Saul would take him prisoner or kill him.

He didn't know the end of the story. He didn't know that Saul would be converted and become Paul, the great missionary. He didn't know about the books Paul would write, the many Paul would lead to Christ, or how God would use Paul to change the world.

All he knew was God said *"go,"* so he went.

Ananias chose to obey God, and the rest is history.

Today, Ananias stands as a reminder to all of us of the potential when we obey the Holy Spirit's call to share our faith with another person.

How often do we think, *"They don't want to hear it," "They have no interest,"* or even *"Do you know the repercussions I may have to face?"*

Yet, what if that person is our Saul?

What if they respond to your testimony, or you are used to plant a seed that ultimately leads to their salvation?

Isn't it worth it?

Ananais reminds us that we are not called to fully understand all of God's plans. We are called to obey God, ride or die.

Today's Verse:

> *In Damascus there was a disciple named Ananias. The Lord called to him in a vision, "Ananias!"*
>
> *"Yes, Lord," he answered.*
>
> *The Lord told him, "Go to the house of Judas on Straight Street and ask for a man from Tarsus named Saul, for he is praying. In a vision he has seen a man named Ananias come and place his hands on him to restore his sight."*

"Lord," Ananias answered, "I have heard many reports about this man and all the harm he has done to your holy people in Jerusalem. And he has come here with authority from the chief priests to arrest all who call on your name."

But the Lord said to Ananias, "Go! This man is my chosen instrument to proclaim my name to the Gentiles and their kings and to the people of Israel. I will show him how much he must suffer for my name."

Then Ananias went to the house and entered it. Placing his hands on Saul, he said, "Brother Saul, the Lord—Jesus, who appeared to you on the road as you were coming here —has sent me so that you may see again and be filled with the Holy Spirit."

Immediately, something like scales fell from Saul's eyes, and he could see again. He got up and was baptized, and after taking some food, he regained his strength. (Acts 9:10-19, NIV)

-Jamie Holden, Founder, Mantour Ministries

Monday

Joshua 5-6 ☐   Psalm 10 ☐

Memory Verse: *Don't be deceived, my dear brothers and sisters. Every good and perfect gift is from above, coming down from the Father of the heavenly lights, who does not change like shifting shadows.* (James 1:16-17, NIV)

Tuesday

Joshua 7-8 ☐   Proverbs 3:1-12 ☐

Memory Verse: *He chose to give us birth through the word of truth, that we might be a kind of firstfruits of all he created.* (James 1:18, NIV)

Wednesday

Joshua 9-10 ☐   Psalm 11 ☐

Memory Verse: *My dear brothers and sisters, take note of this: Everyone should be quick to listen, slow to speak and slow to become angry,* (James 1:19, NIV)

Thursday

Joshua 11 ☐ Joshua 14:6-15 ☐   Joshua 15:13-19 ☐
Proverbs 3:13-20 ☐

Memory Verse: *Because human anger does not produce the righteousness that God desires.* (James 1:20, NIV)

Friday

Joshua 20 ☐   Joshua 22 ☐   Psalm 12 ☐

Memory Verse: *Therefore, get rid of all moral filth and the evil that is so prevalent and humbly accept the word planted in you, which can save you.* (James 1:21, NIV)

Saturday

Joshua 23-24 ☐   Psalm 13 ☐

Memory Verse: *Do not merely listen to the word, and so deceive yourselves. Do what it says.* (James 1:22, NIV)

THOUGHTS AND

REFLECTIONS

-WEEK FOUR-

PASTOR DONALD NOLDER

BY DUANE GOODLING

When I was in elementary school, I had a little book where I could keep my report cards, attach pictures, list friends and write down what I wanted to be when I grew up. Until about third grade, I wrote that I wanted to be an astronaut, football player, or stewardess. Yes, a stewardess. Not sure why, but that's what it says. Then, in fourth grade, it changed. Instead of a stewardess, football player, or astronaut, it changed to just *'scientist.'* For a long time, I wondered what sparked that change.

A few years ago, while going through some old pictures, I found a Christmas picture of me holding up a chemistry set. Looking at the date, I realized that this was during my fourth-grade school year, and when combined with my career goals, it started to make sense. Getting this chemistry set changed my whole outlook.

When I was in high school, I pretty much knew everything. Don't all teens? I wasn't necessarily cocky about it, but I thought I knew pretty much everything I needed to know to be successful in life. However, one area that I would admit that I was naïve was my faith.

The pastor of the church I grew up in was Reverend Donald Nolder or Pastor Don. I only went to church occasionally as a youth, and I didn't pay much attention, so I never really understood a lot of what they sang or talked about. But, as I approached my senior year in high school, Pastor Don asked me to go through the confirmation process to join our church. He felt that I would set a good example for the others because most of them were 13-14 years old and I was

17.   Pastor Don believed in me when I didn't deserve his confidence. I didn't do or say anything to lead him to think I would be a good example; he just believed.   I went through the confirmation process and joined the church.

However, it didn't really mean anything to me. To be completely honest, I only did it because Pastor Don asked me to. I respected him as the pastor, and I felt honored to be asked. I didn't do it because I felt led. Pastor Don also asked if I needed help paying for college. I knew he didn't have money to do much, but that didn't matter.   It was the fact that he even asked and would be willing to sacrifice for me that impacted me. That has always stuck with me, and I've never forgotten his example and willingness to sacrifice for me.

What I didn't recognize at the time was that Pastor Don was acting as a mentor. It was never specified that he was mentoring me; he just lived it. In reality, I'm not sure he would even call it mentoring.   It was just him being him. We need more of these types of people today. People who pour into young people's lives because it is sorely lacking. Pastor Don was setting an example for me and may not have even realized it because he was just living his faith with purpose and integrity.

I was able to thank Pastor Don many years later, albeit through Facebook, because I wanted him to know his impact on my life and my journey into ministry. Just as that chemistry set sparked an interest in science that carried through to college (I was a chemistry major my first two years of college), you could say that Pastor Don did the same. Pastor Don was my living chemistry set, and his influence changed my entire outlook on what it meant to be a person of integrity and faith. He changed my understanding of what it meant to care for and serve others. Today, I am an ordained minister and serve the Lord in many ways.

What impact are you having on others? Trust me; even if you

don't think you are, you are impacting someone with your life. Is it good; is it bad? Is it intentional? I encourage you to be a chemistry set for someone. Help influence someone to change their outlook on life to one of compassion and of faith.

Today's Scripture:

Follow my example, as I follow the example of Christ. (1 Corinthians 11:1, NIV)

-Duane Goodling, Mission Director-Think Missions, www.thinkmissions.org

Monday

Ephesians 1-2 ☐   Psalm 14 ☐

Memory Verse: *Anyone who listens to the word but does not do what it says is like someone who looks at his face in a mirror and, after looking at himself, goes away and immediately forgets what he looks like.* (James 1:23-24, NIV)

Tuesday

Ephesians 3-4 ☐   Proverbs 3:21-35 ☐

Memory Verse: *But whoever looks intently into the perfect law that gives freedom, and continues in it—not forgetting what they have heard, but doing it—they will be blessed in what they do.* (James 1:25, NIV)

Wednesday

Ephesians 5-6 ☐   Psalm 15 ☐

Memory Verse: *Those who consider themselves religious and yet do not keep a tight rein on their tongues deceive themselves, and their religion is worthless.* (James 1:26, NIV)

Thursday

1 Samuel 1-2 ☐   Proverbs 4:1-9 ☐

Memory Verse: *Religion that God our Father accepts as pure and faultless is this: to look after orphans and widows in their distress and to keep oneself from being polluted by the world.* (James 1:27, NIV)

Friday

1 Samuel 3-4 ☐   Psalm 16 ☐

Memory Verse: *My brothers and sisters, believers in our glorious Lord Jesus Christ must not show favoritism.   Suppose a man comes into your meeting wearing a gold ring and fine clothes, and a poor man in filthy old clothes also comes in. If you show special attention to the man wearing fine clothes and say, "Here's a good seat for you," but say to the poor man, "You stand there" or "Sit on the floor by my feet," have you not discriminated among yourselves and become judges with evil thoughts?* (James 2:1-4, NIV)

Saturday

1 Samuel 5-6 ☐   Psalm 17 ☐

Memory Verse: *Listen, my dear brothers and sisters: Has not God chosen those who are poor in the eyes of the world to be rich in faith and to inherit the kingdom he promised those who love him.* (James 2:5, NIV)

-WEEK FIVE-

NOAH
BY JAMIE HOLDEN

Who doesn't love a building project?

Making plans, buying the supplies, grabbing the sledgehammer to start demolition…I can almost hear Tim the Tool Man Taylor grunting now!

Whether you're a professional or weekend do it yourselfer, there's something about a building project that makes us want to grunt along. (Even if we aren't very good at building.)

Sometimes I wonder if Noah didn't let out a little Tool Time grunt when God commanded him to build the ark. Talk about a project! Noah spent years gathering supplies and building the world's first cruise ship before he and his family boarded with two of every kind of animal. This project had to be done right! After all, their lives depended on it, and the fate of humanity depended on their survival.

It was a massive task God gave Noah. Sometimes I wonder how God knew Noah was the right man for the job.

I believe the answer is found in Genesis 6:9:

> *Noah was a righteous man, the only blameless person living on earth at the time, and he walked in close fellowship with God. (Genesis 6:9, NLT)*

Before he was known for the boat, the animals, the flood, and the rainbow, Noah was known as a blameless man who walked in fellowship with God while everyone else rejected God and His ways.

Think about that for a minute.

Noah was one man following God against the culture. He was a ride or die man of God.

When I read this, I thought about all the re-enactments I've seen where the people around Noah think he's crazy for building the boat. If this Scripture is true; then, people thought Noah was crazy and didn't want to be around him long before he picked up a hammer. Noah was always different because he was faithful to God and God's ways.

Even when everyone else around him was living a sinful life, Noah stood out because of His commitment to God.

It was because of this commitment that God saved Noah and his family from the flood.

It's why God knew Noah could be trusted to build the ark according to His instructions, to finish the job and continue humanity's line.

God knew Noah. They had a relationship. Noah had a reputation for following God no matter what everyone else did. That's why he was chosen to build the ark.

Noah's story didn't start when he heard God give him building plans.

It began with his ride or die commitment to having a relationship with God and pursuing a blameless life in a godless world.

If we want to be like Noah, we need to have these same commitments: faithfulness to our relationship with God and a steadfast commitment to His ways.

That's what makes a real man. Can I get a grunt of agreement?

Today's Scripture:

Noah was a righteous man, the only blameless person living on earth at the time, and he walked in close fellowship with God. (Genesis 6:9, NLT)

-Jamie Holden, Founder, Mantour Ministries

Monday

1 Samuel 7-8 ☐   Psalm 18 ☐

Memory Verse: *But you have dishonored the poor. Is it not the rich who are exploiting you? Are they not the ones who are dragging you into court? Are they not the ones who are blaspheming the noble name of him to whom you belong?* (James 2:6-7, NIV)

Tuesday

1 Samuel 9-10 ☐   Proverbs 4:20-27 ☐

Memory Verse: *If you really keep the royal law found in Scripture, "Love your neighbor as yourself," you are doing right.* (James 2:8, NIV)

Wednesday

1 Samuel 11-12 ☐   Psalm 19 ☐

Memory Verse: *But if you show favoritism, you sin and are convicted by the law as lawbreakers.* (James 2:9, NIV)

Thursday

1 Samuel 13-14 ☐   Proverbs 5:1-14 ☐

Memory Verse: *For whoever keeps the whole law and yet stumbles at just one point is guilty of breaking all of it.* (James 2:10, NIV)

Friday

1 Samuel 15-16 ☐   Psalm 20 ☐

Memory Verse: *For he who said, "You shall not commit adultery," also said, "You shall not murder." If you do not commit adultery but do commit murder, you have become a lawbreaker.* (James 2:11, NIV)

Saturday

1 Samuel 17-18 ☐   Psalm 21 ☐

Memory Verse: *Speak and act as those who are going to be judged by the law that gives freedom.* (James 2:12, NIV)

THOUGHTS AND REFLECTIONS

-WEEK SIX-

J.C. LOWMAN
BY WALTER SMITH

With thinning hair, black-rimmed glasses, and smiling from ear to ear, J.C. Lowman drove enthusiastically into the gravel parking lot of the small, paint peeling, run-down church in western North Carolina. His ride was a Ford pickup truck. Light green.

Ole James Cecil warmly greeted my wife and I as the new pastor of the five-member Assemblies of God church. The community believed that the church was closed. However, the faithful few had kept utilities paid over the years in decline. The once thriving church had seen the highs of riding the good times and the rough roads of the lean years.

J.C. Lowman was one of those five members. So when J.C. Lowman drove up, grateful for a very young couple willing to be the pastor, his generosity and warmth overflowed.

For the next six years, it was J.C. that led the prayer for revival. It was J.C. that hoped for new people to attend. It was J.C. who took care of the church finances… in a three-ring notebook. There was no computer software in those days—no QuickBooks. In fact, no computers at all. Even if we did have those modern systems, J.C. Lowman wouldn't have used them. He was country. A simple man. Dedicated wholeheartedly to the work of the Lord. Common sense kind of guy. Honest! One of his favorite sayings to me was, *"Preacher, if Jesus gets 'em saved, He will also save their wallets so they will tithe!"*

It was *"brother"* J.C. Lowman that pushed the pedal to accelerate church growth. He invited people to church. This man of GOD drove the church refurbishing by painting, lawn care, and maintenance of all sorts. It was J.C that encouraged me through difficult days. It was J.C. that rejoiced over people getting saved. It was this man of faith that raised two beautiful daughters all by himself.

It was J.C. Lowman that led me as a young pastor to love people right where they were. He taught me to be compassionate, forgiving, and kind regardless of other individual's responses. It was riding in that truck of J.C.'s that I learned vital lessons in life's journey.

J.C. Lowman taught my wife gardening tips. He was helping her plant the garden, watering tips, assisting her in harvesting potatoes. She had used such great care not to hurt the potato plant by using a kitchen spoon to dig up the 'taters. Ole J.C. pulled out a shovel from the green Ford pickup truck and simply dug up the potatoes. Smiling, he chuckled and said, *"Sister Lynn, this is how we do dig them here!"* Yet it was J.C.'s chuckle paired with his extreme kindness not to embarrass her when he saw this *'city girl'* in action.

It was *"brother"* Lowman's soft demeanor being all things to all men to reach some that impacted my life.

Diligent yet flexible.

Truth matched with love.

Hard work followed by fun.

He was soft-spoken and mostly silent in a large crowd, yet powerful in his words to ignite a spark in anyone's life if they listened to his homespun wisdom.

There is a special place in my life for J.C. Lowman. The mild-mannered, larger-than-life treasurer of our first church pastorate. To this day, I cherish the yellow envelope marked with $17.35 that contained my first week's pay for being their pastor. It was half the offering of my first Sunday as pastor. J.C. Lowman stated just two weeks prior that the church wouldn't be able to pay us anything. Yet, he handed me the envelope with the check and smiled. He was subtly teaching me that we walk by faith and not by sight!

My head still turns when I glimpse an old, light green Ford pickup traveling down the road. Memories instantly flood my head of J.C. Lowman. If only I could take one more ride in that truck to ride with my brother, my mentor. To hear him say just one more time, *"How is it with you preacher?"* What a ride that would be!

Today's Scripture:

For this reason I have sent to you Timothy, my son whom I love, who is faithful in the Lord. He will remind you of my way of life in Christ Jesus, which agrees with what I teach everywhere in every church. (1 Corinthians 4:17, NIV)

-Walter Smith, Retired Pastor, Presbyter, and Founder Men of the Word Ministries

Monday

1 Samuel 19-20☐   Psalm 22 ☐

Memory Verse: *Because judgment without mercy will be shown to anyone who has not been merciful. Mercy triumphs over judgment.* (James 2:13, NIV)

Tuesday

1 Samuel 21-22 ☐   Proverbs 5:15-23 ☐

Memory Verse: *What good is it, my brothers and sisters, if someone claims to have faith but has no deeds? Can such faith save them?* (James 2:14, NIV)

Wednesday

1 Samuel 23-24 ☐   Psalm 23 ☐

Memory Verse: *Suppose a brother or a sister is without clothes and daily food. If one of you says to them, "Go in peace; keep warm and well fed," but does nothing about their physical needs, what good is it?* (James 2:15-16, NIV)

Thursday

1 Samuel 25-26 ☐   Proverbs 6:1-11 ☐

Memory Verse: *In the same way, faith by itself, if it is not accompanied by action, is dead.* (James 2:17, NIV)

Friday

1 Samuel 27-28 ☐   Psalm 24 ☐

Memory Verse: *But someone will say, "You have faith; I have deeds."*

Show me your faith without deeds, and I will show you my faith by my deeds. (James 2:18, NIV)

Saturday

1 Samuel 29-30 ☐   Psalm 25 ☐

Memory Verse: *You believe that there is one God. Good! Even the demons believe that—and shudder.* (James 2:19, NIV)

THOUGHTS AND
REFLECTIONS

-WEEK 7-

ABRAHAM

BY JAMIE HOLDEN

What would your wife say if you told her that God wanted you to pack up everything you could carry, leave your house, community, job, and everything familiar to you, and hit the road?

No hotels or rentals…you'd be living in tents.

Where are you going? Not sure. Wherever God leads. Also, God says He will make you into a great nation even though you don't have any kids and you're really old.

How's it going to happen? Not sure, but God says it will.

Think she'd go for it? Better question, would you?

When we first meet Abraham in Genesis 12, that's exactly what he was doing.

Hebrews 11 puts it this way:

> *"It was by faith that Abraham obeyed when God called him to leave home and go to another land that God would give him as his inheritance. He went without knowing where he was going. And even when he reached the land God promised him, he lived there by faith—for he was like a foreigner, living in tents. And so did Isaac and Jacob, who inherited the same promise." (Hebrews 11:8-9, NLT)*

This alone should prove that Abraham was a ride or die man of God. But his obedience in this area was just the beginning.

The next test would come when God asked Abraham to do

something no man would ever want to do.

Fast forward to Genesis 17, and we see God command Abraham that every male in his household be circumcised as a sign of their covenant. (All God's men cringe in horror.)

Still, Abraham went home and immediately obeyed.

Yet, even this would not be Abraham's biggest test.

That would come years later after Abraham and Sarah were given their promised child. After years of waiting, Isaac is born. They had several years to enjoy him, parent him, and love him when God asked Abraham if he would be willing to sacrifice Isaac to Him.

Now obviously, God never intended for Abraham to sacrifice Isaac. It's against His nature. But Abraham didn't know that. After years of waiting for a son and then years spent living with Isaac, this was Abraham's ultimate *"will you ride or die with Me"* question.

Amazingly, once again, Abraham said *"yes."* Having passed the test, God provided a ram to take Isaac's place.

When it comes to giving up everything to follow God, Abraham was a rock star. He stands as an example for all of us for what it means to be a ride-or-die man is God. We follow his example when we say, *"Whenever, wherever, whatever God asks, the answer will always be 'yes.'"*

Today's Scripture:

By faith Abraham, when God tested him, offered Isaac as a sacrifice. He who had embraced the promises was about to sacrifice his one and only son, even though God had said to him, "It is through Isaac that your offspring will be reckoned." Abraham reasoned that God could even raise the dead, and so in a manner of speaking he did receive Isaac back from death. (Hebrews 11:17-19, NIV)

-Jamie Holden, Founder, Mantour Ministries

Monday

1 Samuel 31 ☐   2 Samuel 1 ☐   Psalm 26 ☐

Memory Verse: *You foolish person, do you want evidence that faith without deeds is useless?* (James 2:20, NIV)

Tuesday

Acts 1-2 ☐   Proverbs 6:12-19 ☐

Memory Verse: *Was not our father Abraham considered righteous for what he did when he offered his son Isaac on the altar?* (James 2:21, NIV)

Wednesday

Acts 3-4 ☐   Psalm 27 ☐

Memory Verse: *You see that his faith and his actions were working together, and his faith was made complete by what he did.* (James 2:22, NIV)

Thursday

Acts 5-6 ☐   Proverbs 6:20-35 ☐

Memory Verse: *And the scripture was fulfilled that says, "Abraham believed God, and it was credited to him as righteousness," and he was called God's friend.* (James 2:23, NIV)

Friday

Acts 7-8 ☐   Psalm 28 ☐

Memory Verse: *You see that a person is considered righteous by what they do and not by faith alone.* (James 2:24, NIV)

Saturday

Acts 9-10 ☐   Psalm 29 ☐

Memory Verse: *In the same way, was not even Rahab the prostitute considered righteous for what she did when she gave lodging to the spies and sent them off in a different direction? As the body without the spirit is dead, so faith without deeds is dead.* (James 2:25-26, NIV)

-WEEK EIGHT-

ZACCHAEUS
BY JOHN LANZA

We all have had these moments in life when what we saw and wanted was out of our reach.

Maybe it is the cookie jar on the countertop as a child or the desire to dunk the basketball as an adolescent or even an adult. The desire is there, but we lack some of the practical components.

Luke writes about a man named Zacchaeus who was facing this same dilemma. (Luke 19)

All that Zacchaeus desired that day was to be able to see Jesus. The whole town was talking about this man, but Zacchaeus did not have much going for him.

As a tax collector, he was not liked by the community and wouldn't get much help from the neighbors. The worst part was that he was short in stature and couldn't see over the crowd. This was an obstacle to overcome.

Zacchaeus could have given up the fight, thrown in the towel, and settled for what he considered the end, desired unfulfilled.

That's not how this story ends. Zacchaeus looked for a solution and found it in a tree. A tree that he climbed and got noticed by the One he desired to see.

Most likely, Zacchaeus didn't know how his day would end, but the impact of His encounter with Jesus not only fulfilled a desire, it changed the course of his life, so much we read about him centuries later.

When you make Christ your Ride or Die, you are giving Him the opportunity to fulfill His desires through and leave a legacy for others to remember.

Look for a tree.

Today's Verse:

Jesus entered Jericho and was passing through. A man was there by the name of Zacchaeus; he was a chief tax collector and was wealthy. He wanted to see who Jesus was, but because he was short he could not see over the crowd. So he ran ahead and climbed a sycamore-fig tree to see him, since Jesus was coming that way.

When Jesus reached the spot, he looked up and said to him, "Zacchaeus, come down immediately. I must stay at your house today." So he came down at once and welcomed him gladly.

All the people saw this and began to mutter, "He has gone to be the guest of a sinner."

But Zacchaeus stood up and said to the Lord, "Look, Lord! Here and now I give half of my possessions to the poor, and if I have cheated anybody out of anything, I will pay back four times the amount."

Jesus said to him, "Today salvation has come to this house, because this man, too, is a son of Abraham. For the Son of Man came to seek and to save the lost." (Luke 19:1-10, NIV)

-John Lanza, Pastor at Glad Tidings Assembly of God, Middletown, PA

Monday

Acts 11-12 ☐   Psalm 30 ☐

Memory Verse: *Not many of you should become teachers, my fellow believers, because you know that we who teach will be judged more strictly.* (James 3:1, NIV)

Tuesday

Acts 13-14 ☐   Proverbs 7:1-5 ☐

Memory Verse: *We all stumble in many ways. Anyone who is never at fault in what they say is perfect, able to keep their whole body in check.* (James 3:2, NIV)

Wednesday

Acts 15-16 ☐   Psalm 31 ☐

Memory Verse: *When we put bits into the mouths of horses to make them obey us, we can turn the whole animal.* (James 3:3, NIV)

Thursday

Acts 17-18 ☐   Proverbs 7:6-27 ☐

Memory Verse: *Or take ships as an example. Although they are so large and are driven by strong winds, they are steered by a very small rudder wherever the pilot wants to go.* (James 3:4, NIV)

Friday

Acts 19-20 ☐   Psalm 32 ☐

Memory Verse: *Likewise, the tongue is a small part of the body, but it makes great boasts. Consider what a great forest is set on fire by a small spark.* (James 3:5, NIV)

Saturday

Acts 21-22 ☐   Psalm 33 ☐

Memory Verse: *The tongue also is a fire, a world of evil among the parts of the body. It corrupts the whole body, sets the whole course of one's life on fire, and is itself set on fire by hell.* (James 3:6, NIV)

THOUGHTS AND REFLECTIONS

-WEEK NINE-

DAVID WILKERSON
BY JAMIE HOLDEN

When I was young, my parents would take my sister and I to the Teen Challenge Training Center in Rehrersburg, PA, for their Friday night graduation ceremonies. I remember seeing the excitement on the men's faces as they shared their testimonies of how Jesus changed their lives and helped them overcome their addiction to drugs and alcohol. I can still hear the families cheering when the men's names were called. They were so proud, excited for a new life, and tremendously thankful for the change Jesus made in the graduates' lives.

Over the years, thousands of men have passed through Teen Challenge Centers across the United States and Canada. Yet, none of this would have been possible without the ride or die attitude of a young country pastor named David Wilkerson.

I'm sure growing up, David Wilkerson never imagined the plans that God had for his life. Born in Indiana, his parents were Pentecostal preachers. He began preaching when he was fourteen years old, attended Central Bible College, and became an Assemblies of God minister in 1952.

Like most ministers of his time, he married shortly after college and began pastoring small churches in Pennsylvania. It seemed like his life would follow a pretty typical pattern. But then the Holy Spirit stepped in and changed everyone's plans.

In his autobiography, *"The Cross and the Switchblade,"* Wilkerson tells how he saw a picture in *Life Magazine* of seven teenagers who were gang members in New York City. The Holy Spirit used this picture to lead Wilkerson to New York and lead these men to Jesus.

Following the Holy Spirit's leading, Wilkerson went to the courtroom where their trial was being held, but he was ejected. This courtroom ruckus led the newspapers to publish Wilkerson's photo.

But this was all part of God's plan. Because of the picture in the paper, the gang members recognized Wilkerson and accepted him when he went to talk to them. He held evangelistic rallies for the gang members, where dozens came to accept Jesus as their Savior. One of the most famous was Nicky Cruz, the leader of the Mau Maus, who went on to be an evangelist and write the book *"Run, Baby, Run."*

Wilkerson founded Teen Challenge Training Centers as a discipleship program for the gang members who came to Christ. Later, he founded World Challenge and Times Square Church.

Over the years, these organizations have played an active role in advancing God's kingdom and helping men and women find hope and healing through Jesus. Yet, it's important to remember that they were all birthed through the obedience of one man who had a ride or die attitude.

Think about it: How many Christians saw that same photo in *Life Magazine* and thought, *"What a pity? Those poor boys."* That wasn't the case for Wilkerson. When he saw the picture, he responded to the Holy Spirit's call to go and take the Gospel to one of the darkest corners of New York City.

Let's be honest. Saying *"yes"* to God's calling to minister to the gangs was dangerous. The book *"Run, Baby, Run"* recounts the heinous practices of this violent and murderous gang. Pastor Wilkerson was literally putting his life on the line to follow God and reach these men.

Still, he went. He answered God's call to ride or die, knowing there was the distinct possibility that he could die.

Today, he stands as an example for everyone who hears God's call to *"go"* to a dangerous or challenging place to spread the Gospel of Jesus. He reminds us that when God calls us, He takes care of us and works out the details so that we can fulfill His plan. He challenges all of us to be brave, to look beyond our little world, and be open to following God beyond anything we can imagine—ride or die.

Today's Scripture:

Then Jesus came to them and said, "All authority in heaven and on earth has been given to me. Therefore go and make disciples of all nations, baptizing them in the name of the Father and of the Son and of the Holy Spirit, and teaching them to obey everything I have commanded you. And surely I am with you always, to the very end of the age." (Matthew 28:18-20, NIV)

-Jamie Holden, Founder, Mantour Ministries

Monday

Acts 23-24 ☐   Psalm 34 ☐

Memory Verse: *All kinds of animals, birds, reptiles and sea creatures are being tamed and have been tamed by mankind, but no human being can tame the tongue. It is a restless evil, full of deadly poison.* (James 3:7-8, NIV)

Tuesday

Acts 25-26 ☐   Proverbs 8:1-11 ☐

Memory Verse: *With the tongue we praise our Lord and Father, and with it we curse human beings, who have been made in God's likeness.* (James 3:9, NIV)

Wednesday

Acts 27-28 ☐   Psalm 35 ☐

Memory Verse: *Out of the same mouth come praise and cursing. My brothers and sisters, this should not be.* (James 3:10, NIV)

Thursday

2 Samuel 2-3 ☐   Proverbs 8:12-21 ☐

Memory Verse: *Can both fresh water and salt water flow from the same spring?* (James 3:11, NIV)

Friday

2 Samuel 4-5 ☐   Psalm 36 ☐

Memory Verse: My brothers and sisters, can a fig tree bear olives, or a grapevine bear figs? Neither can a salt spring produce fresh water. (James 3:12, NIV)

Saturday

2 Samuel 6-7 ☐   Psalm 37 ☐

Memory Verse: *Who is wise and understanding among you? Let them show it by their good life, by deeds done in the humility that comes from wisdom.*   (James 3:13, NIV)

-WEEK TEN-

FAMOUS & NAMELESS: JONATHAN'S ARMOR-BEARER

BY BRAD PRICE

Let's go across to the outpost of those pagans," Jonathan said to his armor bearer. "Perhaps the LORD will help us, for nothing can hinder the LORD. He can win a battle whether he has many warriors or only a few!"

"Do what you think is best," the armor bearer replied. "I'm with you completely, whatever you decide." (1 Samuel 14:6-7, NLT)

Even the toughest of men can't get it done alone. One of the toughest men to ever live, Davy Crockett fought alongside Jim Bowie & William Travis for freedom at the Alamo. Daniel Boone, who could range alone through the wilderness of North America, needed the brotherhood and teamwork of his fellow frontiersman, Simon Kenton. Even the *"Lone"* Ranger had Tonto for crying out loud! You're not going to be able to walk in this world or serve Christ by yourself. Get yourself a brother!

In this portion of Scripture, we're reading about King Saul of Israel. He had a son named Jonathan. Jonathan was tough-as-nails, not some spoiled brat. Jonathan had a famous friend, David. But he also had a comrade in his life of which very few have heard. Even the most die-hard Bible students don't know his name. None of us do! All we know is that he's *"Jonathan's armor-bearer."*

The Kingdom of Israel is at war with Philistia, and Israel's army is vastly outnumbered. Even worse, they are split into two divisions: one with Saul and the other with his young son, Jonathan. You can find this incredible story of faith and daring in 1 Samuel 14.

But things got idled because of King Saul's foolishness. Then his soldiers started slipping away from the army and returning home.

Have you ever been bored… to the point that you get tired of sitting around and you just feel like starting something? Usually, in young men, this is when trouble starts, right?! I mean, this is the part where we get the phone out and make Tik-Toks or Reels! We go after siblings or get into dares or pranks. Jonathan and his armor-bearer were sick of sitting around doing nothing, so they decided to *"get somethin' started!"* Something unheard of…

The Philistine army of at least 9,000 was divided into several factions, and Jonathan felt that he and his armor-bearer could take on one of them by themselves. Not good odds, even on a level playing field. But Jonathan expresses his faith in God's ability to win when he says, *"Let's go to the cliff below them and show ourselves. If they tell us to stay where we are, that's the sign we'll lose. BUT, if they tell us to climb up and fight them, THAT'S the sign that God will give us the win!"* His armor bearer listened to all of this and his response? *"Do what you think is best. I'm with you whatever you decide!"*

I know what I would have been thinking: *"Are you NUTS?! There's twenty of them up there and only TWO of us! AND… there's thousands more RIGHT BEHIND THEM!!!"*

And it hit me! Young Jonathan (most likely a teenager) and his ride or die armor bearer (most likely slightly younger) are brave. Bold. Daring. Loyal.

It's not because they were stupid. It's not because their brains were jacked up from chemicals, steroids, smoke, or even liquids. It's because they had an unswerving faith in the ability of their God, despite how vulnerable they were in this strategic situation. They weren't brave because they had a tactical advantage or superior firepower/weaponry. They knew what their God is capable of!

Read the chapter. They wound up defeating 20. Then panic set in over the entire Philistine army, and it turned into a victory for Israel. All because a guy said, *"Yeah! Let's do it. I'm with ya!"*

What about me? What about you? You might say, *"I don't have a friend like that, a "ride-or-die" buddy".*

Ok, I hear you. Then be one! I've learned in my life that if I want a friend, I have to be a friend... and friendships are for nothing if they don't increase our faith in God's ability to win the day. The overwhelming odds you and I face in life are the same as the cliffs Jonathan & his armor-bearer climbed. So, come on, there are heights to be scaled.

There are battles to be won: for God, not for us! For our lives. For God's Kingdom!

Today's Scripture:

"Let's go across to the outpost of those pagans," Jonathan said to his armor bearer. "Perhaps the LORD will help us, for nothing can hinder the LORD. He can win a battle whether he has many warriors or only a few!"

"Do what you think is best," the armor bearer replied. "I'm with you completely, whatever you decide." (1 Samuel 14:6-7, NLT)

-Brad Price, Pastor Connect Church, Alum Bank, PA

Monday

2 Samuel 8-9 ☐   Psalm 38☐

Memory Verse: *But if you harbor bitter envy and selfish ambition in your hearts, do not boast about it or deny the truth. (James 3:14, NIV)*

Tuesday

2 Samuel 10-11 ☐   Proverbs 8:22-36 ☐

Memory Verse: *Such "wisdom" does not come down from heaven but is earthly, unspiritual, demonic.* (James 3:15, NIV)

Wednesday

2 Samuel 12-13 ☐   Psalm 39 ☐

Memory Verse: *For where you have envy and selfish ambition, there you find disorder and every evil practice.* (James 3:16, NIV)

Thursday

2 Samuel 14-15 ☐   Proverbs 9:1-9 ☐

Memory Verse: *But the wisdom that comes from heaven is first of all pure; then peace-loving, considerate, submissive, full of mercy and good fruit, impartial and sincere.* (James 3:17, NIV)

Friday

2 Samuel 16-18 ☐   Psalm 40 ☐

Memory Verse: *Peacemakers who sow in peace reap a harvest of righteousness.* (James 3:18, NIV)

Saturday

2 Samuel 19-20 ☐   Psalm 41 ☐

Memory Verse: *What causes fights and quarrels among you? Don't they come from your desires that battle within you?* (James 4:1, NIV)

THOUGHTS AND

REFLECTIONS

-WEEK ELEVEN-

MOSES

BY JAMIE HOLDEN

Last Easter, I rewatched the classic movie *"The Ten Commandments"* with Charlton Heston. (Honestly, I'm glad I didn't know how long it was before I started, or my sister would never have agreed to watch it. But once we started, we had to finish.)

I have to admit it was pretty cheesy. Special effects and CGI have come a long way since this film was made, and some parts were downright laughable. I was also surprised how far they drifted from the actual Biblical account of Moses. There were several times we laughingly said, *"That didn't happen."*

But there was one part they got right. As Hebrews 11 tells us, there came the point in Moses' life where he chose to give up all that it meant to be a royal in Egypt to identify with the people of Israel. This choice cost him everything. From prince to shepherd, Moses' life changed because he chose to ride or die with God.

But that's just the beginning of the story. Moses' choice to follow God continued after the burning bush experience when God called him to go back to Egypt and lead His people to the Promised Land. It's one thing to leave a place or position. It's another to go back and tell the greatest power in the world that God is going bring plagues against them for how they treat His people.

Remember: Moses knew these people. He knew the evil in their hearts. He was well aware that, except for God's protection, he was as good as dead. Still, he went.

And God brought the plagues, and eventually, he led the Israelites out of Egypt.

But that still wasn't the end of the story.

Moses' story continues for forty more years as he leads the Israelites through the wilderness…ride or die.

This was no easy task as the Israelites were stubborn, complaining, often faithless people more inclined to go back to Egypt than follow God as Moses led.

Still, in faith, Moses continued to follow God.

His life reminds us that the choice to ride or die with God is more than a one-time event. Although there are burning bush experiences, choosing to follow God whatever it takes means walking with God daily. Good. Bad. Highs and lows. Through the days when the Red Sea parts to the days when you just want to leave all the people in the wilderness to fend for themselves, you keep following God and doing what He calls you to do.

Ride or die.

Today's Verse:

By faith Moses, when he had grown up, refused to be known as the son of Pharaoh's daughter. He chose to be mistreated along with the people of God rather than to enjoy the fleeting pleasures of sin.

He regarded disgrace for the sake of Christ as of greater value than the treasures of Egypt, because he was looking ahead to his reward.

By faith he left Egypt, not fearing the king's anger; he persevered because he saw him who is invisible.

(Hebrews 11:24-29, NIV)

-Jamie Holden, Founder, Mantour Ministries

Monday

2 Samuel 21-22☐   Psalm 42☐

Memory Verse: *You desire but do not have, so you kill. You covet but you cannot get what you want, so you quarrel and fight. You do not have because you do not ask God.* (James 4:2, NIV)

Tuesday

2 Samuel 23-24 ☐   Proverbs 9:10-18 ☐

Memory Verse: *When you ask, you do not receive, because you ask with wrong motives, that you may spend what you get on your pleasures.* (James 4:3, NIV)

Wednesday

Philippians 1-2 ☐   Psalm 43 ☐

Memory Verse: *You adulterous people, don't you know that friendship with the world means enmity against God? Therefore, anyone who chooses to be a friend of the world becomes an enemy of God.* (James 4:4, NIV)

Thursday

Philippians 3-4 ☐   Proverbs 10:1-2 ☐

Memory Verse: *Or do you think Scripture says without reason that he jealously longs for the spirit he has caused to dwell in us?* (James 4:5, NIV)

Friday

Colossians 1-2☐   Psalm 44 ☐

Memory Verse: *But he gives us more grace. That is why Scripture says: "God opposes the proud but shows favor to the humble."* (James 4:6, NIV)

Saturday

Colossians 3-4 ☐   Psalm 45 ☐

Memory Verse: Submit yourselves, then, to God. Resist the devil, and he will flee from you. (James 4:7, NIV)

WEEK TWELVE

JOSEPH
BY TOM SEMBER

Can you imagine waking up one day and hearing that your girlfriend is pregnant, and you've never had relations with her? She is carrying someone else's child, and she tells you that it's the Holy Spirit who got her pregnant!

This is exactly what happened to a guy named Joe. In Matthew's first chapter, we read how an angel of the Lord spoke to him in a dream. The angel told him not to be afraid and even gave him the name of the Child. I wonder if he thought it was just a bad dream, but Joseph, once awake, had a choice to either ride or die!

> *When Joseph woke up, he did what the angel of the Lord had commanded him and took Mary home as his wife. (Matthew 1:24, NIV)*

The definition of ride or die is *"a willingness to do anything for someone you love or someone you appreciate in your life. The person who you stand by in any problem and vice versa,"* [1] This is exactly what Joseph did.

In life, we will face those moments that will rock us to the core, when we must make a choice to either run and hide or be willing to ride and die for the cause. Joseph was ready to die for the woman he loved and the Child that would be born. It didn't matter to him who the father was, only that the woman he loved would have a baby. Joseph's willingness to stand up and marry her and raise Jesus as his own proves that ordinary men can find the strength to ride and die to self and live for Christ.

I must wonder, if we were visited by an angel in our dreams and told what God wanted us to do, would we simply dismiss it and go about our way, or would we stand firm upon God's Word and His promises? Life is about choices, and we live and die by those choices. Joseph had a choice, and he chose to stand by the woman he loved.

There have been times in my life that I wish I had made better choices for the woman I love. I can't go back and re-do my past, but I can make sure that I make choices that bring God honor and show my love to my wife.

We don't read much more about Joseph in God's Word, but we do know that when it came time for him to step up and love Mary and take care of her, he did it!

We read in Matthew 1:19 that Joseph was a righteous man, meaning that he was devoted to the Mosaic Law and lived it. I wonder, if people were to read our life's story, could they say that we are righteous when it comes to how we are devoted to God's Word and live it in such a way that others want to know more about the God we serve?!

We can do things as simple as reading God's Word daily, praying, and getting together with a group of men to talk about life, sharing our struggles, being honest, and loving those we are blessed to have in our life, no matter what we encounter!

In every situation of life, we have the choice to run and hide or ride and die for Jesus. Which do we choose?! Be like Joe and be willing to ride and die for Christ!

Today's Verse:

This is how the birth of Jesus the Messiah came about: His mother Mary was pledged to be married to Joseph, but before they came together, she was found to be pregnant through the Holy Spirit.

Because Joseph her husband was faithful to the law, and yet did not want to expose her to public disgrace, he had in mind to divorce her quietly.

But after he had considered this, an angel of the Lord appeared to him in a dream and said, "Joseph son of David, do not be afraid to take Mary home as your wife, because what is conceived in her is from the Holy Spirit. She will give birth to a son, and you are to give him the name Jesus, because he will save his people from their sins."

.....When Joseph woke up, he did what the angel of the Lord had commanded him and took Mary home as his wife. But he did not consummate their marriage until she gave birth to a son. And he gave him the name Jesus. (Matthew 1:18-21 and 24-25, NIV)

-Tom Sember, www.maletime.org

Monday

1 Kings 1-2 ☐   Psalm 46 ☐

Memory Verse: *Come near to God and he will come near to you. Wash your hands, you sinners, and purify your hearts, you double-minded.* (James 4:8, NIV)

Tuesday

1 Kings 3 ☐   1 Kings 4:20-34 ☐   1 Kings 5 ☐

Proverbs 10:13-21 ☐

Memory Verse: *Grieve, mourn and wail. Change your laughter to mourning and your joy to gloom.* (James 4:9, NIV)

Wednesday

1 Kings 6:11-14 ☐   1 Kings 8-9 ☐   Psalm 47 ☐

Memory Verse: *Humble yourselves before the Lord, and he will lift you up.* (James 4:10, NIV)

Thursday

I Kings 10-11 ☐   Proverbs 10:22-32 ☐

Memory Verse: *Brothers and sisters, do not slander one another. Anyone who speaks against a brother or sister or judges them speaks against the law and judges it. When you judge the law, you are not keeping it, but sitting in judgment on it.* (James 4:11, NIV)

Friday

I Kings 12-13 ☐   Psalm 48 ☐

Memory Verse: *There is only one Lawgiver and Judge, the one who is able to save and destroy. But you—who are you to judge your neighbor?* (James 4:12, NIV)

Saturday

I Kind 14-15 ☐   Psalm 49 ☐

Memory Verse: *Now listen, you who say, "Today or tomorrow we will go to this or that city, spend a year there, carry on business and make money."* (James 4:13, NIV)

-WEEK THIRTEEN-

ELIJAH
BY JAMIE HOLDEN

Sometimes being a ride or die man of God is discouraging.

There are days when you think, *"I have been standing for God and His ways so long. Is it even making a difference?"*

We all go through difficult times that leave us exhausted and questioning our choices.

Living as a ride or die man of God in an ungodly world isn't easy.

Just ask Elijah. He knew.

Have no doubt about it: Elijah was a ride or die man of God. For years, he served as God's prophet, delivering God's messages to a people and a king who didn't want to hear it. Living in the era of Ahab and Jezebel, when many of God's people turned to worshipping Baal, and many of God's prophets were killed or had to go into hiding, Elijah frequently stood against the evil leaders and spoke God's truth.

He was the one who infamously told King Ahab, *"There will be no rain for years because of your sin."* Then he endured the drought and famine, living on God's miraculous provision for him.

Finally, God gave the word and told Elijah it was time for a showdown. He challenged Ahab and the prophets of Baal to a sacrificial dual. The God Who answered with fire would be the god the people would serve.

Like a sportscaster giving highlights, 1 Kings 18 recounts the contest where God decidedly defeats Baal. It was a tremendous victory for God and Elijah.

But the battle left Elijah exhausted. With Jezebel again threatening his life, Elijah fell into deep despair.

Then he went on alone into the wilderness, traveling all day. He sat down under a solitary broom tree and prayed that he might die.

> *"I have had enough, Lord," he said. "Take my life, for I am no better than my ancestors who have already died." (1 Kings 19:4, NLT)*

What? How could this happen? How did Elijah, the great man of God, become so defeated?

Well, he was human. After years of fighting God's battle, he was exhausted.

Notice: God didn't judge him for it.

Instead, God gave him time to rest and recuperate.

During this time, God revealed Himself to Elijah in a new way.

He reminded Elijah that he was not alone.

Finally, he gave him a friend—a protege—a partner in ministry.

For the rest of his life, Elijah had Elisha to help him and encourage him. Elisha continued Elijah's work after he went to Heaven.

I believe this is something we all need to be ride or die men of God. We need friends. We need other godly men in our lives to encourage us, tell us the truth, hold us accountable, and support us in the good times and bad.

Every Elijah needs an Elisha.

We weren't meant to serve God all alone.

We aren't lone rangers; we are part of the body of Christ.

We need other people to support us, challenge us, and help us on our journey to be ride or die men of God.

Today's Scripture:

So Elijah went from there and found Elisha son of Shaphat. He was plowing with twelve yoke of oxen, and he himself was driving the twelfth pair. Elijah went up to him and threw his cloak around him. Elisha then left his oxen and ran after Elijah. "Let me kiss my father and mother goodbye," he said, "and then I will come with you."

"Go back," Elijah replied. "What have I done to you?"

So Elisha left him and went back. He took his yoke of oxen and slaughtered them. He burned the plowing equipment to cook the meat and gave it to the people, and they ate. Then he set out to follow Elijah and became his servant. (1 Kings 19:19-21, NIV)

-Jamie Holden, Founder, Mantour Ministries

Monday

I Kings 16-17 ☐   Psalm 50 ☐

Memory Verse: *Why, you do not even know what will happen tomorrow. What is your life? You are a mist that appears for a little while and then vanishes.* (James 4:14, NIV)

Tuesday

I Kings 18-19 ☐   Proverbs 11:1-11 ☐

Memory Verse: *Instead, you ought to say, "If it is the Lord's will, we will live and do this or that."* (James 4:15,, NIV)

Wednesday

I Kings 20-22 ☐   Psalm 51 ☐

Memory Verse: *As it is, you boast in your arrogant schemes. All such boasting is evil.* (James 4:16, NIV)

Thursday

Mark 1-2 ☐   Proverbs 11:12-19 ☐

Memory Verse: *If anyone, then, knows the good they ought to do and doesn't do it, it is sin for them.* (James 4:17, NIV)

Friday

Mark 3-4 ☐   Psalm 52 ☐

Memory Verse: *Now listen, you rich people, weep and wail because of the misery that is coming on you. Your wealth has rotted, and moths have eaten your clothes.* (James 5:1-2, NIV)

Saturday

Mark 5-6 ☐   Psalm 53 ☐

Memory Verse: *Your gold and silver are corroded. Their corrosion will testify against you and eat your flesh like fire. You have hoarded wealth in the last days.* (James 5:3, NIV)

-WEEK FOURTEEN-

JOHN HARPER: SOUL WINNER
BY SCOTT A. GRAY

Reverend John Harper was a Scottish Baptist pastor who died on April 15th in 1912, with the sinking of the Titanic in the North Atlantic Ocean. He was saved at the age of fourteen and began preaching at eighteen. He pastored Paisley Road Baptist Church in Glasgow, Scotland. The church grew to over 500 people. In his honor, the church was renamed Harper Memorial Baptist Church. He was thirty-nine years old when he boarded the Titanic.

The Titanic was the largest and one of the most luxurious ships in the world. According to *National Geographic*, *"The ship had 16 watertight compartments designed to keep it afloat if damaged. This led to the belief that the ship was unsinkable."* Pastor Harper, who was a widower at the time, was traveling with his six-year-old daughter and niece to preach at the Moody Church in Chicago for several weeks. Unfortunately, the ship hit an iceberg, and it sank.

On that night, 1,528 people drowned in the frigid waters. Pastor John Harper put his only daughter and his niece on a lifeboat and began to swim to people in the water, preaching the Gospel and leading them to Jesus, just before the hypothermia would claim his life. The story has been told that Pastor Harper swam up to a young man who was floating on a piece of debris. Pastor Harper asked him point-blank, *"Are you saved?"* The young man replied that he was not saved.

Pastor Harper persisted in leading him to Christ, but the young man still refused to believe in Jesus. He then took off his life jacket and threw it to the man and said, *"Here then, you need this more than I do..."* and swam away to other people.

A few minutes later, Pastor Harper swam back to the young man and succeeded in leading him to salvation. Of the 1,528 people that went into the water that night, only six were rescued by the lifeboats. This young man was one of the six who was rescued from floating on the debris. It was several years later, at a survivor's meeting, this young man stood up with tears streaming down his face and shared about how Pastor John Harper had led him to Christ.

Pastor Harper had tried to swim back to lead other people to Christ, but his body became too weak to swim because of the hypothermia. The survivors who witnessed the actions of Pastor Harper said that his last words before drowning were from Acts 16:31, **"Believe in the name of the Lord Jesus, and you will be saved."**

This man of God exemplified a ride or die commitment to Christ. While other people were trying to get onto the lifeboats to save their own lives, Pastor John Harper laid down his life so that others could be saved before they perished in the frigid water.

Pastor John Harper knew the urgency of winning souls to Christ. He was God's ride or die pastor and evangelist! You should be inspired to evangelize the lost at every opportunity you are given by God, even when you face losing your own life. The apostle Paul wrote to the church in Ephesus with these succinct and persuasive words, in Ephesians 5:15-16.

Today's Scripture:

"Be very careful, then, how you live—not as unwise but as wise, making the most of every opportunity, because the days are evil." (Ephesians 5:15-16, NIV)

-Scott A. Gray, Associate Pastor, Lighthouse Church

Monday

Mark 7-8 ☐   Psalm 54 ☐

Memory Verse: *Look! The wages you failed to pay the workers who mowed your fields are crying out against you. The cries of the harvesters have reached the ears of the Lord Almighty.* (James 5:4, NIV)

Tuesday

Mark 9-10 ☐   Proverbs 11:20-31 ☐

Memory Verse: *You have lived on earth in luxury and self-indulgence. You have fattened yourselves in the day of slaughter.* (James 5:5, NIV)

Wednesday

Mark 11-12 ☐   Psalm 55 ☐

Memory Verse: *You have condemned and murdered the innocent one, who was not opposing you* (James 5:6, NIV)

Thursday

Mark 13-14 ☐   Proverbs 12:1-13 ☐

Memory Verse: *Be patient, then, brothers and sisters, until the Lord's coming. See how the farmer waits for the land to yield its valuable crop, patiently waiting for the autumn and spring rains.* (James 5:7, NIV)

Friday

Mark 15-16 ☐   Psalm 56 ☐

Memory Verse: *You too, be patient and stand firm, because the Lord's coming is near.* (James 5:8, NIV)

Saturday

2 Kings 1-2 ☐   Psalm 57 ☐

Memory Verse: *Don't grumble against one another, brothers and sisters, or you will be judged. The Judge is standing at the door! (James 5:9, NIV)*

-WEEK FIFTEEN-

SHADRACH, MESCHACH, ABENDIGO
BY JAMIE HOLDEN

Even when the king said, *"Bow or I'll throw you into the fiery furnace"…. (Daniel 3:14-15)*

Even when they made the furnace ten times hotter—so hot that even the men who were escorting them to the furnace died from the heat. (Daniel 3:19-20)

Shadrach, Meshach, and Abednego said, *"Ride or die. We won't bow."*

It's important to recognize that for Shadrach, Meschach, and Abednego, the possibility of death was very, very high. Like 99.9%. The only hope they had was that God would come through and do a miracle. When these three men made their choice, there was no guarantee this would happen. (They hadn't read the end of the story.)

Still, with no guarantee and the high probability of death by incineration, these ride or die men made this commitment: ***"If we are thrown into the blazing furnace, the God we serve is able to deliver us from it, and he will deliver us from Your Majesty's hand. But even if he does not, we want you to know, Your Majesty, that we will not serve your gods or worship the image of gold you have set up." (Daniel 3:17-18, NIV)***

"But even if He does not"….

What a powerful statement! Now that's ride or die.

It stands as an example for all of us committed to being ride or die men of God…no matter what happens.

Whether God does a miracle or we suffer consequences for our stand for Christ, we will still follow Him.

As we make this commitment, we have the promise that just as Jesus was in the fire with these three young men, He will be right there with us through it all. It is not guaranteed that the fire won't touch us. However, we can always believe His words that He will never leave us or forsake us (Hebrews 13:5), that the Holy Spirit will give us the words we should speak (Luke 12:11-12), and that ride or die, He will be with us as we are with Him to the end of the line.

Today's Scripture:

Shadrach, Meshach and Abednego replied to him, "King Nebuchadnezzar, we do not need to defend ourselves before you in this matter. If we are thrown into the blazing furnace, the God we serve is able to deliver us from it, and he will deliver us from Your Majesty's hand.

But even if he does not, we want you to know, Your Majesty, that we will not serve your gods or worship the image of gold you have set up." (Daniel 3:16-18, NIV)

-Jamie Holden, Founder, Mantour Ministries

Monday

2 Kings 3-4 ☐   Psalm 58☐

Memory Verse: *Brothers and sisters, as an example of patience in the face of suffering, take the prophets who spoke in the name of the Lord.* (James 5:10, NIV)

Tuesday

2 Kings 5-6 ☐   Proverbs 12:14-28 ☐

Memory Verse: *As you know, we count as blessed those who have persevered. You have heard of Job's perseverance and have seen what the Lord finally brought about. The Lord is full of compassion and mercy.* (James 5:11, NIV)

Wednesday

2 Kings 7-8 ☐   Psalm 59 ☐

Memory Verse: *Above all, my brothers and sisters, do not swear—not by heaven or by earth or by anything else. All you need to say is a simple "Yes" or "No." Otherwise you will be condemned.* (James 5:12, NIV)

Thursday

2 Kings 9-10 ☐   Proverbs 13:1-8 ☐

Memory Verse: *Is anyone among you in trouble? Let them pray. Is anyone happy? Let them sing songs of praise.* (James 5:13, NIV)

Friday

2 Kings 11-12 ☐   Psalm 60 ☐

Memory Verse: *Is anyone among you sick? Let them call the elders of the church to pray over them and anoint them with oil in the name of the Lord.* (James 5:14, NIV)

Saturday

2 Kings 13-14 ☐   Psalm 61 ☐

Memory Verse: *And the prayer offered in faith will make the sick person well; the Lord will raise them up. If they have sinned, they will be forgiven.* (James 5:15, NIV)

-WEEK SIXTEEN-

RIDE OR DIE FOR YOUR LOCAL CHURCH
BY TOM REES

I grew up in Philly and loved the Rocky movies, but the greatest Rocky story is found in the Bible.

> *Simon Peter and the disciples were talking about the rumors of who Jesus was when Simon Peter answered, "You are the Christ, the Son of the living God."*
>
> *Jesus replied, "Blessed are you, Simon son of Jonah! For this was not revealed to you by flesh and blood, but by My Father in heaven. And I tell you that you are Peter, and on this rock I will build My church, and the gates of Hades will not overcome it..." (Matthew 16:17-18, NIV)*

The church wasn't to be built on Simon Peter but on the revelation of who Jesus is. Two thousand years later, that revelation of who Jesus is, conveyed through the local church, is still igniting lives!

We all have a story of how we came to Christ and the church. This is mine...

I remember in school they would have you draw your family tree. Mine was a family shrub. I have had three dads in my life.

Dad #1 disappeared from my life when he and my Mom were divorced when I was a preschooler. It wasn't until nearly two decades later that I reunited with him.

Dad #2 was a helicopter pilot and was killed in action when I was in elementary school.

Dad #3 was an attorney for an oil company. As a high schooler, I looked up to him as a mentor until we found out the truth about his secret life. He had multiple mistresses and affairs.

Mom was devastated and reached out to my Uncle Joe to confront him in front of his weekend family. As we drove through the neighborhood, he was in the driveway and, with a look of panic, directed us to meet him down the road.

When we arrived in a parking lot, he came running towards us. I warned my uncle that he knew karate. That is when my uncle opened up the trunk and grabbed the tire iron.

Mom saw this heading in the wrong direction and pleaded with my uncle to let him go. As he ran away, we were left in that parking lot with anger, betrayal, and loss.

But we were in the parking lot of a church…

My mom went inside, and in that brief conversation, she was encouraged to give it all to Jesus. Her life was changed that day. Six months later, I became a Christian as well.

That is why I believe in your church and starting new ones. It's why I work toward the vision to see 100 new churches planted in five years.

Why? Because the message of the local church is the hope of the world.

As men of God, we need to be ride or die for our local church as it fulfills Jesus' mission to seek and to save the lost. Through our involvement as men, our churches will be stronger and more missional as we serve, give and lead.

Your world needs your local church, and your local church needs you to be committed to it—ride or die.

Today's Scripture:

Jesus replied, "Blessed are you, Simon son of Jonah! For this was not revealed to you by flesh and blood, but by My Father in heaven. And I tell you that you are Peter, and on this rock I will build My church, and the gates of Hades will not overcome it…" *(Matthew 16:17-18, NIV)*

-PennDel Ministry Network Men's Ministry Director and Home Missions Director

Monday

2 Kings 15-16 ☐   Psalm 62 ☐

Memory Verse: *Therefore confess your sins to each other and pray for each other so that you may be healed. The prayer of a righteous person is powerful and effective.* (James 5:16, NIV)

Tuesday

2 Kings 17-18 ☐   Proverbs 13:9-15 ☐

Memory Verse: *Elijah was a human being, even as we are. He prayed earnestly that it would not rain, and it did not rain on the land for three and a half years.* (James 5:17, NIV)

Wednesday

2 Kings 19-20 ☐   Psalm 63 ☐

Memory Verse: *Again he prayed, and the heavens gave rain, and the earth produced its crops.* (James 5:18, NIV)

Thursday

2 Kings 21-23 ☐   Proverbs 13:16-20 ☐

Memory Verse: *My brothers and sisters, if one of you should wander from the truth and someone should bring that person back.* (James 5:19, NIV)

Friday

2 Kings 24-25 ☐   Psalm 64 ☐

Memory Verse: *Remember this: Whoever turns a sinner from the error of their way will save them from death and cover over a multitude of sin.* (James 5:20, NIV)

Saturday

Galatians 1-2 ☐   Proverbs 13:21-25 ☐

Memory Verse: *Peter, an apostle of Jesus Christ, To God's elect, exiles scattered throughout the provinces of Pontus, Galatia, Cappadocia, Asia and Bithynia, who have been chosen according to the foreknowledge of God the Father, through the sanctifying work of the Spirit, to be obedient to Jesus Christ and sprinkled with his blood:*

Grace and peace be yours in abundance. (1 Peter 1:1-2, NIV)

THOUGHTS AND

REFLECTIONS

-WEEK SEVENTEEN-

DANIEL
BY JAMIE HOLDEN

We can't have a book about men who choose to ride or die for God without talking about Daniel.

Why? Because, as we read in the prophetic book named after him, he was literally faced with this choice over and over again as he worked for several crazy kings.

For instance, there was the time that crazy King Nebuchadnezzar said to all of his noblemen (Daniel included), *"Tell me what I dreamt and what it means or die!!"*

Now obviously, no one could do that. Dream interpretation is one thing, but knowing what someone dreams is not possible. Unless God tells you the dream. Entering into emergency prayer, Daniel and his friends prayed, and God told Daniel the dream.

Then there was the time King Belshazzar threw a wild party and defiled the things dedicated to God's temple. Who did they call when the hand appeared to write a message on the wall? Yep, our boy Daniel. Once again, God gave him the interpretation, and that night Daniel's words were fulfilled when King Darius conquered King Belshazzar's kingdom. However, Daniel was not killed or taken captive. Instead, Darius made him the third highest ruler in the kingdom.

Then came the biggest and probably most infamous challenge of Daniel's life. Being hated by his fellow noblemen, they set a trap designed explicitly for Daniel. Knowing his commitment to God and prayer, they convinced King Darius to make a law saying that people could only pray to him for a month. If anyone was caught praying to anyone or anything else, they were thrown into the lion's den.

What did Daniel do?   He chose once again to ride or die with God.

He prayed and was thrown into the lion's den.

Once again, God saved his life, and the lions didn't eat him. Again, Daniel stood with God, and God was faithful to him.

Do you ever wonder what gave Daniel the motivation to choose to face the lions rather than just obey the king's edict?

The key is found in Daniel 6:10. It's what he's always done.

Starting way back in his teens, Daniel faced a challenge: eat food that was against God's laws or obey the king.   Living in a new land under a king who had no fear of God, it was unthinkable for four Hebrews to say, *"We have to obey God no matter what happens."*

Yet, that's what Daniel and his friends did.   When they chose to ride or die to obey God's Laws, they saw God honor them.   This strengthened their faith and gave them the confidence in God to choose His ways again and again.

Often it is the same with us.   Each time we choose to obey God, no matter the consequences, it builds our faith and prepares us for the next challenge.   That's why it's so important that we follow God in the little things.   Choose faithfulness to God in every area of our lives.

Just as every compromise creates a fault line that weakens your walk with God, every time you choose to stand firm, to obey God, to ride or die with Him strengthens and shores up the foundation of your faith.

When the storms of life come, your ability to stand firm will be determined by the foundation you've laid.   Will your foundation be weak from compromise or strong and stable from a history of choosing to ride or die for God?

Daniel could face the lion's den because he had a history of obeying God.

Today's the day to start building your history: choose to obey God.

Today's Verse:

Now when Daniel learned that the decree had been published, he went home to his upstairs room where the windows opened toward Jerusalem. Three times a day he got down on his knees and prayed, giving thanks to his God, just as he had done before. (Daniel 6:10, NIV)

-Jamie Holden, Founder, Mantour Ministries

Monday

Galatians 3-4 ☐   Psalm 65 ☐

Memory Verse: *Praise be to the God and Father of our Lord Jesus Christ! In his great mercy he has given us new birth into a living hope through the resurrection of Jesus Christ from the dead,* (1 Peter 1:3, NIV)

Tuesday

Galatians 5-6 ☐   Proverbs 14:1-9 ☐

Memory Verse: *And into an inheritance that can never perish, spoil or fade. This inheritance is kept in heaven for you.* (1 Peter 1:4, NIV)

Wednesday

Titus 1-3 ☐   Psalm 66 ☐

Memory Verse: *Who through faith are shielded by God's power until the coming of the salvation that is ready to be revealed in the last time.* (1 Peter 1:5, NIV)

Thursday

Ruth 1-2 ☐   Proverbs 14:10-18 ☐

Memory Verse: *In all this you greatly rejoice, though now for a little while you may have had to suffer grief in all kinds of trials.* (1 Peter 1:6, NIV)

Friday

Ruth 3-4 ☐   Psalm 67 ☐

Memory Verse: *These have come so that the proven genuineness of your faith—of greater worth than gold, which perishes even though refined by fire—may result in praise, glory and honor when Jesus Christ is revealed.* (1 Peter 1:7, NIV)

Saturday

Jonah 1-2 ☐   Psalm 68 ☐

Memory Verse: *Though you have not seen him, you love him; and even though you do not see him now, you believe in him and are filled with an inexpressible and glorious joy, for you are receiving the end result of your faith, the salvation of your souls.* (1 Peter 1:8-9, NIV)

THOUGHTS AND REFLECTIONS

-WEEK EIGHTEEN-

JOHN THE BAPTIST...THE GREATEST MAN WHO EVER LIVED!

BY DAN COURTNEY

Jesus said this about John, *"I tell you the truth, of all who have ever lived, none is greater than John the Baptist." (Matthew 11:11a - NLT)*

What a statement! The greatest man who ever lived! You thought that was Jesus, didn't you? Well, of course, it was, but since Jesus was talking, He picked someone else. So who was John the Baptist? What made him so great?

John the Baptist was an interesting dude, that's for sure. He was the homeless man of his day. He wore the same clothes all the time, lived in the wild, ate locusts and honey, but there was more. He was a man on a mission, and he had become the most popular man in the entire region. People traveled for days to come and hear him preach at the Jordan River. And John was the first one to master altar calls. When John spoke, he was direct and demanding, calling people to repent of their sins! People came forward in droves to give their lives to God and get baptized in the Jordan River. The religious leaders came out to hear him. He even had an audience with King Herod himself. He was a powerful, popular man!

But wait a minute, the world has seen many powerful, popular speakers...even preachers. This doesn't seem like something that would make him the greatest man who ever lived. If not this, what was it?

I think John's greatness comes down to him fulfilling his real purpose in life...which was to pave the way for the Messiah. There was a prophecy that was hundreds of years old from Isaiah, *"Listen! It's the voice of someone shouting, 'Clear the way through the wilderness for the Lord! Make a straight highway through the wasteland for our God!'" (Isaiah 40:3, NLT)* This was a prophecy about the Messiah, and John was the fulfillment of this prophecy.

I want you to remember John's purpose: to pave the way for Jesus. I'll come back to it. The end of that fulfillment came after John was sure that Jesus was the Messiah. He said, *"He must become greater and greater, and I must become less and less." (John 3:30, NLT)*

Think about someone with incredible popularity and fame that they worked so hard for...and then at the very peak of success, just to lay it all down and allow someone else to move into the spotlight. That is incredibly hard. Jesus recognized this! This was not the action of a normal man...this is a part of what made John the greatest man who ever lived.

But the other part that made him so great was that his purpose was not just for him. In fact, I think that when Jesus told us that John was the greatest man who ever lived, what He was really saying was, *"Do like John did. Follow his example."*

John was great because he was our example. The purpose he fulfilled was the same purpose we are all called to...to pave the way for Jesus to be known by others as the Messiah that He is. When we do this, we are fulfilling the purpose of John the Baptist, which is also OUR purpose. And to let Jesus shine, we must first decrease so that He can increase.

So how are you doing with this? Is Jesus shining through in your life? Are there people in your life that need to know Jesus? List them in the journal section.

If we really want Jesus to be known by the people in our lives, maybe we need to pray a prayer like this one: *"Lord Jesus, I want Uou to shine in my life. So please help me to understand how I can become less so You can become more. Help me to remember my purpose and pave the way for the people in my life to know YOU. And Holy Spirit, empower me to be a bold witness of all that Jesus has been for me. In Jesus' name, amen."*

Today's Scripture:

He said, "He must become greater and greater, and I must become less and less." (John 3:30, NLT)

-Dan Courtney, Pastor,
https://www.youtube.com/c/DevotionswithDan

Monday

Jonah 3-4 ☐   Psalm 69 ☐

Memory Verse: *Concerning this salvation, the prophets, who spoke of the grace that was to come to you, searched intently and with the greatest care,* (1 Peter 1:10, NIV)

Tuesday

Romans 1-2 ☐   Proverbs 14:19-35 ☐

Memory Verse: *Trying to find out the time and circumstances to which the Spirit of Christ in them was pointing when he predicted the sufferings of the Messiah and the glories that would follow.* (1 Peter 1:11, NIV)

Wednesday

Romans 3-4 ☐   Psalm 70 ☐

Memory Verse: *It was revealed to them that they were not serving themselves but you, when they spoke of the things that have now been told you by those who have preached the gospel to you by the Holy Spirit sent from heaven. Even angels long to look into these things.* (1 Peter 1:12, NIV)

Thursday

Romans 5-6 ☐   Proverbs 15:1-9 ☐

Memory Verse: *Therefore, with minds that are alert and fully sober, set your hope on the grace to be brought to you when Jesus Christ is revealed at his coming.* (1 Peter 1:13, NIV)

Friday

Romans 7-8 ☐   Psalm 71 ☐

Memory Verse: *As obedient children, do not conform to the evil desires you had when you lived in ignorance.* (1 Peter 1:14, NIV)

Saturday

Romans 9-10 ☐   Psalm 72 ☐

Memory Verse: *But just as he who called you is holy, so be holy in all you do; for for it is written: "Be holy, because I am holy."* (1 Peter 1:15-16, NIV)

THOUGHTS AND

REFLECTIONS

-WEEK NINETEEN-

MICAIAH
BY JAMIE HOLDEN

If you follow professional golf, you know that intense rivalries are nothing new.

There was Jack Nicholas and Tom Watson.

Greg Norman and Nick Faldo.

Tiger Woods and Phil Michelson.

2021 added the names Brooks Koepka and Bryson DeChambeau to the mix. Last summer, everyone who watched golf knew these guys hated each other. They didn't even try to hide it. For instance, during one interview, DeChambeau walked behind Koepka while he was being interviewed. Completely overcome by annoyance, Koepka lost his train of thought, rolled his eyes, and disgustedly blurted out some expletives that were beeped by television. It was amusing to watch as sports shows played it over and over again.

I think of that scene whenever I read about King Ahab's reaction to the prophet Micaiah. I imagine King Ahab making the same face at just the mention of the prophet's name.

In case you aren't familiar, here's the story.

Ahab was king of Israel, and Jehosophat was king of Judah. Ahab wanted Jehosophat to accompany him into a battle. Although he inititally agreed, on second thought, Jehosophat said maybe they should consult the Lord before heading off to war.

Trying to convince Jehosophat to be his ally, Ahab called in a bunch of *"yes men"* who called themselves prophets. They predicted victory all around for the two kings. Still, King Jehosophat wasn't convinced, and he asked if there was a prophet of the Lord they could consult.

Here's where I think King Ahab did his best Brookes Koepka impersonation:

> *The king of Israel answered Jehoshaphat, "There is still one prophet through whom we can inquire of the Lord, but I hate him because he never prophesies anything good about me, but always bad. He is Micaiah son of Imlah."*
>
> *"The king should not say such a thing," Jehoshaphat replied.*
>
> *So the king of Israel called one of his officials and said, "Bring Micaiah son of Imlah at once." (1 Kings 22:8-9, NIV)*

So Micaiah shows up, and as King Ahab predicted, he tells the king the truth: God has predicted Ahab's doom.

King Ahab loses it and says, *"Put this man in prison, and feed him nothing but bread and water until I return safely from the battle!"*

Micaiah declared, *"If you ever return safely, the Lord has not spoken through me." Then he added, "Mark my words, all you people!" (1 Kings 22:28, NIV)*

Spoiler Alert: King Ahab died in the battle. We are left to assume that Micaiah lived the rest of his life eating bread and water in prison. (Because Ahab's son was also a wicked king.)

Yet, even knowing this would be his fate, Micaiah didn't back down. Having a ride or die commitment to speaking God's truth as God's prophet, he gave God's message to the king.

Today, he stands as an example to us of how we can be ride or die men of God in a world that doesn't want to hear God's truth. Living in a culture that doesn't want to hear the truth about salvation, Heaven, Hell, or sin, are we willing to make personal sacrifices to speak God's truth? Will we be like Micaiah or like the *"yes men"* who said what would benefit them?

Granted, few of us will stand before kings, but each day we come in contact with people who need to hear the truth that they don't want to hear. Will we love them enough to speak the truth in our families, in our communities, at our jobs, or even in our churches?

Will we represent God no matter what—ride or die?

Today's Scripture:

But Micaiah said, "As surely as the Lord lives, I can tell him only what the Lord tells me." (1 Kings 22:14, NIV)

-Jamie Holden, Founder, Mantour Ministries

Monday

Romans 11-12☐   Psalm 73 ☐

Memory Verse: *Since you call on a Father who judges each person's work impartially, live out your time as foreigners here in reverent fear.* (1 Peter 1:17, NIV)

Tuesday

Romans 13-14☐   Proverbs 15:10-18 ☐

Memory Verse: *For you know that it was not with perishable things such as silver or gold that you were redeemed from the empty way of life handed down to you from your ancestors,* (1 Peter 1:18, NIV)

Wednesday

Romans 15-16☐   Psalm 74 ☐

Memory Verse: *But with the precious blood of Christ, a lamb without blemish or defect.* (1 Peter 1:19, NIV)

Thursday

Ezra 1-2☐   Proverbs 15:15-24 ☐

Memory Verse: *He was chosen before the creation of the world, but was revealed in these last times for your sake.* (1 Peter 1:20, NIV)

Friday

Ezra 3-4☐   Psalm 75 ☐

Memory Verse: *Through him you believe in God, who raised him from the dead and glorified him, and so your faith and hope are in God.* (1 Peter 1:21, NIV)

Saturday

Ezra 5-6 ☐   Psalm 76 ☐

Memory Verse: *Now that you have purified yourselves by obeying the truth so that you have sincere love for each other, love one another deeply, from the heart.* (1 Peter 1:22, NIV)

-WEEK TWENTY-

THE STORY OF BASANT
BY DUANE GOODLING

We often hear stories of people who face tremendous adversity in life because of their faith, but they often seem abstract, and we may have difficulty relating to them. But they do happen every day all around the world. An example of this is my friend, Basant.

Basant Lama was born in 1978 and lives in West Bengal, India. Basant was born into a very devout Buddhist family; however, as a young boy, he was sent to a Christian school because it offered a better education than the public schools. Basant heard many Bible stories of Moses, Abraham, King David, and Jesus Christ at that school.

In February 1993, Basant's mother had a severe stroke, and after a few days, she passed away. It was a very painful and dark time in his life because he was left alone in a house with a drunk father. All his siblings were married and had gone to start their own families in other places, so Basant had no one to depend on.

Basant had no peace in his life and was very lonely. However, one day he received an invitation from a teacher, who was also a pastor, to attend a small prayer fellowship. He was able to go, and it was there where God first touched his life while the preacher was sharing the Word of God from Luke 19:1-10 about Jesus and Zacchaeus. In this story, Jesus calls Zacchaeus by his name, which resonated with Basant. It was there where Basant found the love of Christ.

Basant gave his life to Jesus Christ and accepted Him as his personal Lord and Saviour in 1993. But his father did not like his decision to follow Jesus Christ. He kicked Basant out of his house and left him with nothing. Though his father rejected him, he knew he remained highly favored and loved by God. Basant had to drop out of school, but was able to go to a sister's house and stay there for few months. He was water baptized, and by the grace of God, he was able to go to a Bible school in the large city of Delhi in July 1994. After completing Bible school, he continued to stay in Delhi for a little over five years, ministering and helping to plant five churches.

In obedience to God's voice, Basant returned to West Bengal in November 1999, but there was no room to stay with family. He rented a house in a village called Oodlabari and started a church planting ministry. Basant was married in February 2008. Since then, he and his wife, Shrijana, were blessed with a son and a daughter.

It was very difficult, but the Holy Spirit convicted Basant, and through obedience, he was able to forgive his father after many years. This reconciliation was initiated by a gift of a sweater and blanket to his father as winter approached. Basant and his wife then brought his father to live with them until his last breath in 2019. His father, along with almost all of his family, has accepted Jesus Christ as their personal Savior.

I was honored to have met Basant's father before his passing. He was such a gentle soul that I cannot imagine him being the person he was before Christ. He was a life changed by the power of Christ and the Holy Spirit. He couldn't do much at his advanced age and had difficulty hearing, but he would sit and watch us work for hours. It was comforting to see him there. He is greatly missed.

Much of what I have written so far comes from Basant's own words, but he left out many of the struggles and persecution he faced along the way. When he told his father he accepted Christ, his father slapped him in the face before kicking him out, and when Basant was thirty-one years old, some men took his motorcycle and burned it because he was a Christian. There are many difficulties for Christians in India, but in Basant's own words: *"God has been so faithful and kind to me. He is leading me step by step in the ministry. By the grace of God, my wife, son, daughter, and I are doing well, and the ministry that the Lord has entrusted to us is growing. God is good all the time!"*

As Christians, we may experience verbal or possibly even physical persecution, but it is often mild compared with what those in other areas of the world face. I truly believe that Basant and his ministry have been blessed because of his obedience and his focus always being outwards, on others and not himself. Years ago, Basant created a list of ten things that he wanted to accomplish with his life and ministry. All of them were outward-focused and based on serving Christ and others except two: having a wife and providing a home for his wife. I don't think we could argue with those two.

Basant's ministry provides food, training, and faith for those in and around his home village. He serves as a wonderful example of obedience and faith in the face of adversity, and I am honored to call him my friend.

Today's Scripture:

Blessed are you when people insult you, persecute you and falsely say all kinds of evil against you because of me. Rejoice and be glad, because great is your reward in heaven, for in the same way they persecuted the prophets who were before you. (Matthew 5:11-12, NIV)

-Duane Goodling, Mission Director- Think Missions, www.thinkmissions.org

Monday

Ezra 7-8 ☐   Psalm 77 ☐

Memory Verse: *For you have been born again, not of perishable seed, but of imperishable, through the living and enduring word of God.* (1 Peter 1:23, NIV)

Tuesday

Ezra 9-10 ☐   Proverbs 15:25-33 ☐

Memory Verse: *For, "All people are like grass, and all their glory is like the flowers of the field; the grass withers and the flowers fall,* (1 Peter 1:24, NIV)

Wednesday

Nehemiah 1-2 ☐   Psalm 78 ☐

Memory Verse: *But the word of the Lord endures forever." And this is the word that was preached to you.* (1 Peter 1:25, NIV)

Thursday

Nehemiah 4-5 ☐   Proverbs 16:1-5 ☐

Memory Verse: *Therefore, rid yourselves of all malice and all deceit, hypocrisy, envy, and slander of every kind.* (1 Peter 2:1, NIV)

Friday

Nehemiah 6-7:1-3 ☐   Nehemiah 8☐   Psalm 79 ☐

Memory Verse: *Like newborn babies, crave pure spiritual milk, so that by it you may grow up in your salvation, now that you have tasted that the Lord is good.* (1 Peter 2:2-3, NIV)

Saturday

Nehemiah 9 and 10:28-37 ☐   Psalm 80 ☐

Memory Verse: *As you come to him, the living Stone—rejected by humans but chosen by God and precious to him.*   (1 Peter 2:4, NIV)

-WEEK TWENTY-ONE-

MORDECAI
BY JAMIE HOLDEN

Fan's of 90's sitcoms will readily recognize the name Steve Urkel, the lovable, accident-prone nerd next door on Family Matters. It was almost guaranteed that if something was breakable in a scene when Urkel entered the room, he'd find a way to destroy it and then utter his catchphrase, *"Did I do that?"* Then everyone in the room glared at him disgustedly as if to say, *"Yes, you did that."* It's a classic comedy.

Having watched this show a million times, this phrase came to my mind the other day, and I wondered if that's how the people of Israel looked at Mordecai when the king's edict came down. Because realistically, the king's edict that all of the Jews be slaughtered was Mordecai's fault. Yes, he did that.

Let's recap.

Mordecai is one of the main characters in the book of Esther. He was Esther's uncle, but he raised her as his own after her parent's died. Like the other Jews of their time, they lived as exiles in Susa. Even though Mordecai lived in a foreign land, he chose to obey God's Laws and ride or die. This included the law that says you should not bow to anyone but God.

Mordecai's refusal to bow drove one of the king's noblemen, Haman, absolutely insane! Why? Because everyone bowed down to him, EXCEPT Mordecai. Haman couldn't stand him. In fact, it bothered Haman so much that he went to King Xerxes, lied about the

Jewish people, and had the king put out a mandate that all of the Jews would be killed on a specific day. All because one man wouldn't bow, can you believe it?

Yet, this was the truth the Jewish people faced….and it was all Mordecai's fault.

So Mordecai went to now Queen Esther and said, *"You have to do something."*

Esther said, *"I'd be putting my life on the line…can't do it."*

Then came the infamous line, *"Who knows if perhaps you were made queen for just such a time as this?"*

At first read, it seems odd that Mordecai asked Esther to put her life on the line for a problem he created. And yet, thinking further, I realized that Mordecai loved Esther. He didn't want to see harm come to her. He spent his days outside the palace so he could watch over her. When Mordecai asked Esther to take responsibility, he knew that if something happened to her, HE would feel the loss because he loved her.

At great sacrifice to him and those he loved, Mordecai chose to take responsibility to see the fight his stand created through to the end.

He led the Jews in a time of intercessory prayer, and then he sent the one he loved most in the world to plead their case.

As we know, God came through for His people and saved them from destruction.

As I read this passage in this light, we can see a fundamental truth: There are times when we take a stand for righteousness or choose to obey God that things don't turn out the way we plan. People don't always respect our intentions. There isn't always a happy ending. Often a man of God who stands for righteousness makes people angry. That anger sparks persecution.

We see this happen more and more in our society. Christians stand for their beliefs, but rather than riding off like heroes into the sunset, they face difficult consequences. Some lose family members or friends. Others lose jobs. Some face lawsuits that drag on for years and years.

Mordecai challenges us to obey God no matter the repercussions, follow through, and continue standing during the implications. Be prepared that sometimes the choice to ride or die with God may bring personal loss. Acknowledge that these battles will have to be fought through intercessory prayer while you hold your ground. Be inspired by Mordecai to never back down and recognize that perhaps YOU were called into the kingdom to take this stand and fight this battle—ride or die.

Today's Scripture:

When Esther's words were reported to Mordecai, he sent back this answer: "Do not think that because you are in the king's house you alone of all the Jews will escape. For if you remain silent at this time, relief and deliverance for the Jews will arise from another place, but you and your father's family will perish. And who knows but that you have come to your royal position for such a time as this?"

Then Esther sent this reply to Mordecai: "Go, gather together all the Jews who are in Susa, and fast for me. Do not eat or drink for three days, night or day. I and my attendants will fast as you do. When this is done, I will go to the king, even though it is against the law. And if I perish, I perish."

So Mordecai went away and carried out all of Esther's instructions. (Esther 4:12-17, NIV)

-Jamie Holden, Founder, Mantour Ministries

Monday

Nehemiah 11:27-47 ☐   Nehemiah 13 ☐   Psalm 81 ☐

Memory Verse: *You also, like living stones, are being built into a spiritual house to be a holy priesthood, offering spiritual sacrifices acceptable to God through Jesus Christ.* (1 Peter 2:5, NIV)

Tuesday

I Timothy 1-2 ☐   Proverbs 16:16-24 ☐

Memory Verse: *For in Scripture it says: "See, I lay a stone in Zion, a chosen and precious cornerstone, and the one who trusts in him will never be put to shame."* (1 Peter 2:6, NIV)

Wednesday

I Timothy 3-4 ☐   Psalm 82 ☐

Memory Verse: *Now to you who believe, this stone is precious. But to those who do not believe, "The stone the builders rejected has become the cornerstone,"* (1 Peter 2:7, NIV)

Thursday

I Timothy 5-6 ☐   Proverbs 16:25-33 ☐

Memory Verse: *And, "A stone that causes people to stumble and a rock that makes them fall." They stumble because they disobey the message— which is also what they were destined for.* (1 Peter 2:8, NIV)

Friday

2 Timothy 1-2 ☐   Psalm 83 ☐

Memory Verse: *But you are a chosen people, a royal priesthood, a holy nation, God's special possession, that you may declare the praises of him who called you out of darkness into his wonderful light.* (1 Peter 2:9, NIV)

Saturday

2 Timothy 3-4 ☐   Psalm 84 ☐

Memory Verse: *Once you were not a people, but now you are the people of God; once you had not received mercy, but now you have received mercy.* (1 Peter 2:10, NIV)

-WEEK TWENTY-TWO-

A CHIROPRACTOR'S CALLING
BY JAMIE HOLDEN

It was the worst night of our lives. One minute we were laughing with our Mom, and the next, she collapsed and died without warning. Having been shuffled out of the room by the EMTs, Adessa called Mom's long-time doctor, Gerry Dincher. Over the years, he went above and beyond taking care of Mom, helping her deal with very severe environmental allergies, and giving her the treatment she needed. He often came in at night or on the weekend to help open her lungs when they were shutting down or help control her vertigo. When the insurance company deemed chiropractic care *"unnecessary,"* he saw her and us at a reduced cash rate so she could still get the care she needed.

We always knew he was a good man, but I came to admire him in new ways that night. Knowing the difficult situation we'd been living in with our Dad, and how close we were to our Mom, he did something that night that changed our lives. It was 6 p.m. when Adessa called him. He'd just put in a full day of seeing patients and had to be tired. Still, he drove two hours in one of the worst storms I can remember to meet us at the hospital.

That night, he drove us home and tried to speak words of comfort and hope to our devastated hearts. The two things I remember most are that he rolled up the sleeves on his dress shirt and washed our dishes before the relatives came, and he cleaned up all of the mess the EMTs left so we wouldn't have to see it.

He helped us through the funeral, and over the next few years, he was there for us every time we needed someone to step into the advisor role. I don't know how we would have made it through that time without him. He was a God-send, stepping into a situation where he had no obligation and showing love and direction as we walked through this difficult time.

This isn't just something he did for us. He's quietly helped so many people taking on the role of servant, helper, and advisor over the years. It's just who he is.

A few years ago, he went through his own personal tragedy when one of his sons suddenly died in his early thirties. It was a heartbreaking time for his whole family. Even though I know it broke his heart, he did not turn away from God as many others have in similar situations. Instead, he continued being who he is: a man of faith and conviction who loves God, loves his family, and does what he can to show love to people.

While most will never know his name, he has changed so many lives by getting up every day and exemplifying what it means to be a man of God—through good times and bad—ride or die.

I'm grateful to know him. He's a truly ride or die man of God.

Today's Scripture:

Those who have served well gain an excellent standing and great assurance in their faith in Christ Jesus. (1 Timothy 3:13, NIV)

-Jamie Holden, Founder, Mantour Ministries

Monday

Esther 1-2 ☐   Psalm 85 ☐

Memory Verse: *Dear friends, I urge you, as foreigners and exiles, to abstain from sinful desires, which wage war against your soul.* (1 Peter 2:11, NIV)

Tuesday

Esther 3-4 ☐   Proverbs 17:1-11 ☐

Memory Verse: *Live such good lives among the pagans that, though they accuse you of doing wrong, they may see your good deeds and glorify God on the day he visits us.* (1 Peter 2:12, NIV)

Wednesday

Esther 5-6 ☐   Psalm 86 ☐

Memory Verse: *Submit yourselves for the Lord's sake to every human authority: whether to the emperor, as the supreme authority, or to governors, who are sent by him to punish those who do wrong and to commend those who do right.* (1 Peter 2:13-14, NIV)

Thursday

Esther 7-8 ☐   Proverbs 17:12-20 ☐

Memory Verse: *For it is God's will that by doing good you should silence the ignorant talk of foolish people.* (1 Peter 2:15, NIV)

Friday

Esther 9-10 ☐   Psalm 87 ☐

Memory Verse: *Live as free people, but do not use your freedom as a cover-up for evil; live as God's slaves.* (1 Peter 2:16, NIV)

Saturday

Philemon 1 ☐   James 1 ☐   Psalm 88 ☐

Memory Verse: *Show proper respect to everyone, love the family of believers, fear God, honor the emperor.* (1 Peter 2:17, NIV)

THOUGHTS AND

REFLECTIONS

-WEEK TWENTY-THREE-

JOSEPH
BY JAMIE HOLDEN

Next year I will have officially been holding Men's Conferences for close to a decade. I've been attending them even longer. As far as I can remember, I have never been to a men's event that did not talk about sexual purity.

I understand why. Whether sex outside of marriage, adultery, pornography, or any other sexual sin, a commitment to Biblical sexuality is a struggle for many guys. Yet, the Bible is clear that part of being a ride or die, man of God, is maintaining a radical commitment to Biblical purity.

One man who sets the standard for this is Joseph.

Most of us have heard the story.

Joseph was Jacob's favorite son. He's a little spoiled, and his brothers all hate him for it. Their hatred is so extreme that they sell him to an Egyptian caravan and tell their father he died. That's some pretty intense hatred!

But God still had plans for Joseph, and when he got to Egypt, he was sold to a high-ranking government official named Potiphar. Because he was blessed by God and a really hard worker, Joseph rose through the ranks until he was in charge of everything in Potiphar's house.

While Joseph was going about his life faithfully doing his duty, sexual temptation came his way. The Bible tells us that Joseph was a stud (ok, it doesn't say it exactly that way, but it's what is implied), and he caught the eye of Potiphar's wife. Being used to getting everything she wanted, she propositioned him over and over again.

When Joseph declined her offer, she went so far as to set a trap where they would be alone together. If he accepted, no one would know. This time she took her proposition further than ever before, making it almost impossible for him to say *"no."*

Yet, Joseph maintained Biblical purity. Genesis 39:9 give us his motivation: ***"How could I do such a wicked thing? It would be a great sin against God." (NLT)***

Joseph refused Potiphar's wife's invitation because he was ride or die for His God. Even though God let him be sold into slavery, even though the temptation was tremendous, Joseph held fast in His commitment to living by God's ways.

Today, he challenges all of us to follow his example when faced with sexual temptation. While most of us don't have beautiful women throwing themselves at us every day, we live in a world where sexual temptation is prevalent. It's easy to believe the lie that sexual sin is normal for men, that no one will ever find out, and even if they do, everyone else is doing it, too.

Some men even believe that God is okay with their sexual sin. Progressive Christianity teaches that all forms of sexuality are beautiful and acceptable in God's eyes. However, this is not true. In the New Testament, 1 Thessalonians 4:3 says, ***"God's will is for you to be holy, so stay away from all sexual sin." (NLT)***

Like Joseph, we need to choose whether we want to be holy men of God or be men who entertain and participate in sexual sin. You can't have it both ways.

One of the practical ways that we can choose to be ride or die men of God is to choose to stay away from all sexual sin. We need to do whatever it takes to live pure and holy lives before God.

We need to understand that God takes sex seriously. He designed it to be between one man and one woman who are married to each other. Like Joseph, we need to run away from all other sexual opportunities simply because we don't want to sin against God.

Today's Scripture:

Run from sexual sin! No other sin so clearly affects the body as this one does. For sexual immorality is a sin against your own body. Don't you realize that your body is the temple of the Holy Spirit, who lives in you and was given to you by God? You do not belong to yourself, for God bought you with a high price. So you must honor God with your body. (1 Corinthians 6:18-20, NLT)

-Jamie Holden, Founder, Mantour Ministries

Monday

James 2-3 ☐   Psalm 89 ☐

Memory Verse: *Slaves, in reverent fear of God submit yourselves to your masters, not only to those who are good and considerate, but also to those who are harsh.* (1 Peter 2:18, NIV)

Tuesday

James 4-5 ☐   Proverbs 17:21-28 ☐

Memory Verse: *For it is commendable if someone bears up under the pain of unjust suffering because they are conscious of God.* (1 Peter 2:19, NIV)

Wednesday

Ecclesiastes 1-2 ☐   Psalm 90 ☐

Memory Verse: *But how is it to your credit if you receive a beating for doing wrong and endure it? But if you suffer for doing good and you endure it, this is commendable before God.* (1 Peter 2:20, NIV)

Thursday

Ecclesiastes 3-4 ☐   Proverbs 18:1-8 ☐

Memory Verse: *To this you were called, because Christ suffered for you, leaving you an example, that you should follow in his steps.* (1 Peter 2:21, NIV)

Friday

Ecclesiastes 5-6 ☐   Psalm 91 ☐

Memory Verse: *"He committed no sin, and no deceit was found in his mouth."* (1 Peter 2:22, NIV)

Saturday

Ecclesiastes 7-8 ☐   Psalm 92 ☐

Memory Verse: *When they hurled their insults at him, he did not retaliate; when he suffered, he made no threats. Instead, he entrusted himself to him who judges justly.* (1 Peter 2:23, NIV)

FRANKLIN "BUD" STOVER: RIDE WITH CONFIDENCE...DIE WITH DIGNITY

BY JIM PENTZ

In my office, there is a picture that spans four generations. I look at that picture just about every day. The four generations are my father-in-law, me, my two sons-in-law, and my grandson. It speaks to me of legacy, running the good race, and passing the torch from one generation to the next.

Psalm 145:4 reads, *"One generation will commend your works to another; they will tell of your mighty acts."* (NIV)

In that picture is a man that I had the privilege to follow, and two men and a boy I have the responsibility to lead. For me, he was, and for them, I want to be a *"Ride or Die Man of God."*

Allow me to share the testimony of my father-in-law, Franklin *"Bud"* Stover. When Bud was sixteen, he didn't play sports or hang out after school like his classmates. He drove an empty coal truck to the mines, had it loaded with coal, and drove it back down the mountain so his father could unload it the next day while Bud was in school.

As a teenager, he entered the military to fight in World War II. Bud drove a munitions truck, often behind the enemy lines so the infantry would have what they needed to engage the enemy in the fight of their lives. Once, Bud was separated from his troop. He stopped in a European town to ask where his troop was last seen. He was directed down a windy road through a valley and told they might be in the hills on the other side. Upon arriving on the other side, there were no signs of his comrades, so Bud turned the truck around and drove through the valley, back into town. Upon entering the town, he was told that the road he had passed through twice was full of land mines. Bud accredited God with keeping him safe and directing his truck.

After the war, Bud drove trucks for most of his life. He drove in and out of difficult places, worked on his own truck, and provided for his family. His driving skills impressed state troopers as he backed his rig up along the interstate to pick up a load off a wrecked trailer. He also impressed dock workers as he maneuvered his truck down alleys to loading docks in downtown Philadelphia. But the most impressive thing I ever saw Bud do, he did while on his death bed. As his body was being ravaged with cancer and his life on this earth was nearing an end, the hospice doctor asked him if he knew what was happening to him.

Bud replied, *"Well, I am dying in phases."*

The doctor asked, *"How do you feel about that?"*

Bud answered, *"There is no sense getting emotional about it."*

The doctor asked, *"How are you able to say that? What is giving you that confidence?"*

Bud replied, *"My faith in God. My faith in Jesus."* Then he did something that was such a *"Ride or Die Man of God"* moment.

He sat up in his bed, looked straight into the eyes of the doctor, and asked, *"Doc, do you believe?"*

When the doctor said that he did, Bud laid back in his bed and simply said, *"Good."* It wasn't long after that Bud went to be with his

Lord.

In his life, he rode with confidence. In his death, he died with dignity, knowing that a better world awaited him. That is the kind of legacy I want to pass on to the generations that follow me. Let's all of us strive to be *"ride or die men of God."*

Questions to consider:

Who are you following? Why are you following them?

Who are you leading? How are you leading them?

Today's Scripture:

One generation will commend your works to another; they will tell of your mighty acts. (Psalm 145:4, NIV)

-Jim Pentz, Lead Pastor, New Covenant Assembly of God, Montgomery, PA, Presbyter, North Central Section, PennDel Ministry Network

Monday

Ecclesiastes 9-10 ☐   Psalm 93 ☐

Memory Verse: *Wives, in the same way submit yourselves to your own husbands so that, if any of them do not believe the word, they may be won over without words by the behavior of their wives, when they see the purity and reverence of your lives.* (1 Peter 3:1-2, NIV)

Tuesday

Ecclesiastes 11-12 ☐   Proverbs 18:9-19 ☐

Memory Verse: *Your beauty should not come from outward adornment, such as elaborate hairstyles and the wearing of gold jewelry or fine clothes. Rather, it should be that of your inner self, the unfading beauty of a gentle and quiet spirit, which is of great worth in God's sight. (1 Peter 3:3-4, NIV)*

Wednesday

1 Thessalonians 1-2 ☐   Psalm 94 ☐

Memory Verse: *For this is the way the holy women of the past who put their hope in God used to adorn themselves. They submitted themselves to their own husbands, like Sarah, who obeyed Abraham and called him her lord. You are her daughters if you do what is right and do not give way to fear.* (1 Peter 3:5-6, NIV)

Thursday

1 Thessalonians 3-4 ☐   Proverbs 18:20-24 ☐

Memory Verse: *Husbands, in the same way be considerate as you live with your wives, and treat them with respect as the weaker partner and as heirs with you of the gracious gift of life, so that nothing will hinder your prayers.* (1 Peter 3:7, NIV)

Friday

1 Thessalonians 5 ☐   2 Thessalonians 1 ☐   Psalm 95 ☐

Memory Verse: *Finally, all of you, be like-minded, be sympathetic, love one another, be compassionate and humble.* (1 Peter 3:8, NIV)

Saturday

2 Thessalonians 2-3 ☐   Psalm 96 ☐

Memory Verse: *Do not repay evil with evil or insult with insult. On the contrary, repay evil with blessing, because to this you were called so that you may inherit a blessing.* (1 Peter 3:9, NIV)

THOUGHTS AND

REFLECTIONS

-WEEK TWENTY-FIVE-

JOSIAH
BY JAMIE HOLDEN

When I was in my late twenties, we visited a church where the pastor challenged his congregation to have a *"Josiah Day."* For those who don't know what this means, Josiah was one of the good kings in Israel. He followed God with all of his heart and obeyed all of God's commands.

Josiah didn't follow just a little—no, he was EXTREME in his obedience.

Why? Because he knew that up until then, his people were EXTREME in their disobedience.

As we read in 2 Kings 22, one day while they were working in the Temple, the Book of the Law was found. As soon as it was read to Josiah, it wrecked him. He was brought to tears and tore his robe seeing how far God's people were living from God's ways.

So he sent for the prophetess, who basically said, *"I'm sorry, but it's too late. God is going to judge His people for their sins. But it won't happen in your lifetime."*

At this point, Josiah could have done a few things. He could have seen the situation as hopeless and thought, *"Nothing I can do."* He could have taken a deep breath and said, *"At least it won't happen to me."*

Instead, he rolled up his sleeves and got to work getting rid of

ALL idol worship and every single thing associated with idol worship in his kingdom. Read the chapter and see that he was EXTREME—getting rid of EVERY SINGLE THING that was against God's Law.

Then, he got God's Temple back in shape and re-instituted the proper practices for worshiping God that were abandoned long ago. He led the people in celebrating the Passover and did all that he could to get the people back on track.

2 Kings 23:25 describes him this way: ***"Neither before nor after Josiah was there a king like him who turned to the Lord as he did —with all his heart and with all his soul and with all his strength, in accordance with all the Law of Moses."***

Today, King Josiah sets an example that many of us need to follow as we commit to being ride or die men of God.

It is time for us to go through our lives, through our hearts, maybe even through our houses, and get rid of everything that doesn't please God. It's time for us to stop saying, *"Well, everyone else is doing it. No one else has a problem with it."* We need to stop making excuses for our sin and compromise and go to extremes in passionate obedience to God.

It's time to get rid of books, magazines, internet sites, television shows, movies, hobbies, habits, or anything else that is displeasing to God. We need to abandon anything connected with the occult, magic, witchcraft, yoga, or any foreign religion. It's time we stopped playing around with pornography and say, *"Once and for all, it's out of here."* It could be alcohol or an especially violent video game. Really, the possibilities are endless of sinful things that Christians entertain that should be abolished from their lives.

It's time to go all Josiah and get them out of our lives once and for all!

Then we need to commit to ride or die, implementing true spiritual disciplines into our lives. We need a fresh commitment to prayer, Bible reading, and Bible study.

It's time to make a ride or die commitment to obeying God and abandoning disobedience. It's time for a Josiah day.

Today's Scripture:

Then the king called together all the elders of Judah and Jerusalem.

He went up to the temple of the Lord with the people of Judah, the inhabitants of Jerusalem, the priests and the prophets—all the people from the least to the greatest. He read in their hearing all the words of the Book of the Covenant, which had been found in the temple of the Lord.

The king stood by the pillar and renewed the covenant in the presence of the Lord—to follow the Lord and keep his commands, statutes and decrees with all his heart and all his soul, thus confirming the words of the covenant written in this book. Then all the people pledged themselves to the covenant. (2 Kings 23:1-3, NIV)

-Jamie Holden, Founder, Mantour Ministries

Monday

Judges 1-3☐   Psalm 97 ☐

Memory Verse: *For, "Whoever would love life and see good days must keep their tongue from evil and their lips from deceitful speech."* (1 Peter 3:10, NIV)

Tuesday

Judges 4-5 ☐   Proverbs 19:1-7 ☐

Memory Verse: *They must turn from evil and do good; they must seek peace and pursue it.* (1 Peter 3:11, NIV)

Wednesday

Judges 6-7 ☐   Psalm 98 ☐

Memory Verse: *"For the eyes of the Lord are on the righteous and his ears are attentive to their prayer, but the face of the Lord is against those who do evil."* (1 Peter 3:12, NIV)

Thursday

Judges 8-9 ☐   Proverbs 19:8-15 ☐

Memory Verse: *Who is going to harm you if you are eager to do good? But even if you should suffer for what is right, you are blessed. "Do not fear their threats; do not be frightened."* (1 Peter 3:13-14, NIV)

Friday

Judges 10-12 ☐   Psalm 99 ☐

Memory Verse: *But in your hearts revere Christ as Lord. Always be prepared to give an answer to everyone who asks you to give the reason for the hope that you have. But do this with gentleness and respect,* (1 Peter 3:15, NIV)

Saturday

Judges 13-14 ☐   Psalm 100 ☐

Memory Verse: *Keeping a clear conscience, so that those who speak maliciously against your good behavior in Christ may be ashamed of their slander.* (1 Peter 3:16, NIV)

-WEEK TWENTY-SIX-

BOOKER T WASHINGTON
BY CORNELIUS MURPHY

I recently read a biography on Booker T. Washington, the founder of Tuskegee University in Alabama. With racial tension in our society being so high, I wanted to get a perspective from someone who lived through slavery at the height of racial tensions. As a black man, I found the biography, *"Up From Slavery"* to be encouraging.

Booker T. Washington was raised on a slave plantation yet excelled in leadership and was well known and respected in both the black and white community. His success was not based on his color, but on his character and devotion to the education and advancement of the black community.

Booker T. Washington seized the opportunity to take classes between shifts while working for a salt furnace after his family was freed from slavery through the Emancipation Proclamation. Washington's own determination to better himself forged attributes in his character that would help others persevere adversity as well.

Washington recites his journey to Hampton Institute in Virginia. While traveling to his destination, Washington ran out of money in Richmond. He slept under a sidewalk at night and secured a job loading cargo ships for money in the daytime. Washington was determined to pursue his dream of obtaining an education, whatever it takes.

The trials and tribulations Booker T. Washington endured are emblematic of challenges in life that we can encounter. Granted, we may not undergo the same struggles that Washington faced, but life will be filled with challenges. The question is will we meet those challenges or surrender to them.

As people of faith, we don't rely on our own strength, but the strength we find in God. Somehow God always makes a way. Somehow God always shows up in the middle of our challenges.

Looking at the life of Booker T. Washington, who was a man of faith, you see the divine hand of God. For example, Washington took a position to clean the home of a prominent family in West Virginia. The lady he worked for taught him good work ethics and how to maintain a home well. When Washington arrived at the Hampton Institution, the teacher of assignments gave him a broom and told him to clean the recitation room. Washington gives credit to the training he received in West Virginia learning to clean well for his acceptance into the Hampton Institution. In a way, it showed his values and worth to the institution.

The divine hand of God works in tandem with our willingness to act. Philippians 2:13 states, *"For God is working in you, giving you the desire and the power to do what pleases him." (NLT)* The godly ambitions and desires we have come from the Lord. However, we have a part in causing the ambitions and desires to come to past.

After receiving his education from the Hampton Institute and spending some time teaching in his hometown of West Virginia, Booker T. Washington accepted a position to teach in Tuskegee, Alabama. Washington taught students in a small shanty and a vacant church building.

Soon the school expanded, and a hen house was cleaned and utilized as a classroom. Washington was a hard worker, which inspired others to join his efforts. Washington's work ethics and dedication were the cornerstones of the school. In fact, the buildings erected on the grounds of the Tuskegee Institution were built by attending students. Students also harvested crops essential for food.

Washington shares this thought regarding pursuing dreams and ambitions, *"In order to be successful in any kind of undertaking, I think the main thing is for one to grow to the point where he completely forgets himself; that is, to lose himself in a great cause."*[1]

This advice is similar to the Apostle Paul's advice to his young protégé Timothy in 1 Timothy 4:15, ***"Give your complete attention to these matters. Throw yourself into your tasks so that everyone will see your progress." (NLT)***

In summary, God works and in and through us to accomplish His good purpose. For us, we must be dedicated to seeing that purpose through. Give it what it takes.

Today's Scripture:

For God is working in you, giving you the desire and the power to do what pleases him. (Philippians 2:13, NLT)

-Cornelius Murphy, C.A.R.E. Director, Calvary Chuch Dover, DE

Monday

Judges 15-16 ☐   Psalm 101 ☐

Memory Verse: *For it is better, if it is God's will, to suffer for doing good than for doing evil.* (1 Peter 3:17, NIV)

Tuesday

Judges 17-18 ☐   Proverbs 19:16-29 ☐

Memory Verse: *For Christ also suffered once for sins, the righteous for the unrighteous, to bring you to God. He was put to death in the body but made alive in the Spirit.* (1 Peter 3:18, NIV)

Wednesday

Judges 19-21 ☐   Psalm 102:1-17 ☐

Memory Verse: *After being made alive, he went and made proclamation to the imprisoned spirits,* (1 Peter 3:19, NIV)

Thursday

Luke 1-2 ☐   Proverbs 20:1-10 ☐

Memory Verse: *To those who were disobedient long ago when God waited patiently in the days of Noah while the ark was being built. In it only a few people, eight in all, were saved through water,* (1 Peter 3:20, NIV)

Friday

Luke 3-4 ☐   Psalm 102:18-28 ☐

Memory Verse: And this water symbolizes baptism that now saves you also —not the removal of dirt from the body but the pledge of a clear conscience toward God. It saves you by the resurrection of Jesus Christ, (1 Peter 3:21, NIV)

Saturday

Luke 5-6 ☐   Psalm 103 ☐

Memory Verse: *Who has gone into heaven and is at God's right hand—with angels, authorities and powers in submission to him.* (1 Peter 3:22, NIV)

-WEEK TWENTY-SEVEN-

FOUR FISHERMEN
BY JAMIE HOLDEN

The other day I stopped to ask directions from an older man fishing with his grandson. It was a familiar scene. A young boy was fishing with his father or grandfather...passing down the tradition of an afternoon at the lake. Carrying poles and buckets, they were headed back to their car with the one fish they'd caught at the lake.

As I drove on, the scene reminded me of another group of fishermen who spent not only hours but days and years on the lake with their father and maybe their grandfather. For them, fishing wasn't a hobby; it was a way of life. It was how they earned their living and fed their family. Passed down through the generations, fishing was part of their identity. They probably hoped to pass the business down to their sons. They were fishermen.

Jesus called out to them, ***"Come, follow me, and I will show you how to fish for people!"*** (Matthew 4:19, NLT)

It was the invitation of the ages—an invitation to be a disciple of the Man John the Baptist had just declared was the Messiah.

But it wasn't a part-time commitment. Following Jesus would mean giving up the life they knew, the security, the family business.

It was a ride or die moment. Would they follow Jesus or keep fishing?

Matthew 4:18-22 tells us that Peter, Andrew, James, and John:

"left their nets at once and followed him." (Matthew 4:20, NLT)

Their story stands in sharp contrast to the rich young ruler who was given the same offer but walked away sad because he couldn't give up all he had to gain more than he could imagine.

These fishermen challenge all of us to examine ourselves and determine whether we will follow their example and give up everything to follow Jesus. One of the problems with modern Christians is that while these men walked away from everything to follow Jesus, many Christians today won't give up anything to follow Him.

When the Holy Spirit says, *"Walk away from this sin, this habit, this hobby, this relationship, or this security,"* each of us needs to follow the example of Peter, Andrew, James, and John and say, *"I'm on it— right away."*

Like their commitment, our obedience needs to be immediate.

Whatever You want, Lord, I'll abandon anything for You and commit to anything You ask.

Today's Scripture:

One day as Jesus was walking along the shore of the Sea of Galilee, he saw two brothers—Simon, also called Peter, and Andrew—throwing a net into the water, for they fished for a living.

Jesus called out to them, "Come, follow me, and I will show you how to fish for people!" And they left their nets at once and followed him.

A little farther up the shore he saw two other brothers, James and John, sitting in a boat with their father, Zebedee, repairing their nets. And he called them to come, too. They immediately followed him, leaving the boat and their father behind. (Matthew 4:18-22, NIV)

-Jamie Holden, Founder, Mantour Ministries

Monday

Luke 7-8 ☐   Psalm 104 ☐

Memory Verse: *Therefore, since Christ suffered in his body, arm yourselves also with the same attitude, because whoever suffers in the body is done with sin.* (1 Peter 4:1, NIV)

Tuesday

Luke 9-10 ☐   Proverbs 20:11-18 ☐

Memory Verse: *As a result, they do not live the rest of their earthly lives for evil human desires, but rather for the will of God.* (1 Peter 4:2, NIV)

Wednesday

Luke 11-12 ☐   Psalm 105 ☐

Memory Verse: *For you have spent enough time in the past doing what pagans choose to do—living in debauchery, lust, drunkenness, orgies, carousing and detestable idolatry.* (1 Peter 4:3, NIV)

Thursday

Luke 13-14 ☐   Proverbs 20:19-30 ☐

Memory Verse: *They are surprised that you do not join them in their reckless, wild living, and they heap abuse on you.* (1 Peter 4:4, NIV)

Friday

Luke 15-16 ☐   Psalm 106 ☐

Memory Verse: *But they will have to give account to him who is ready to judge the living and the dead.* (1 Peter 4:5, NIV)

Saturday

Luke 17-18 ☐   Psalm 107 ☐

Memory Verse: *For this is the reason the gospel was preached even to those who are now dead, so that they might be judged according to human standards in regard to the body, but live according to God in regard to the spirit.* (1 Peter 4:6, NIV)

-WEEK TWENTY-EIGHT-

LARRY TITUS AND BOB KAPP
BY JAMIE HOLDEN

I was only two years old when my Mom became a born again Christian, and our family began attending a small church in our town.   For the first few years, my parents loved it.   They were involved in everything, and they basked in the feeling of community in their new Christian family.

Everything was good until there was a pastoral change.   The new pastor brought with him a scandal that ended in the church splitting. Although I was too young to remember, because Adessa is MUCH older (really only three years, but I like to tease her), she remembers a lot.   It was brutal!   Because my parents were so involved and my Dad was on every committee, she saw and heard all of the ugliness as people who were once friends now chose sides and devoured each other.

Eventually, that pastor left, but things didn't get better.   By the time we left when I was eleven, the church went through several splits, the people endured a lot of abuse by leaders, and we'd seen far too much hypocrisy by men who acted one way in church and treated their families differently behind closed doors.

Adessa often says that by the time she was thirteen, she knew she loved Jesus, but didn't have much to say for the church.

Thankfully, our Mom followed the advice of a former pastor and said, *"Enough.   We're finding another church."*   Our search led us to

Christ Community Church in Camp Hill, PA, where we met Pastor Larry Titus and his youth pastor, Pastor Bob Kapp.

Adessa will tell you for her, she loved this church immediately. As soon as we attended our first service, she knew there was something different about this place. Over the next decade, these two men modeled for us how to do Christianity and ministry well.

They were men of integrity—committed to doing things honestly and truthfully.

They modeled generosity, not just encouraging people to give, but practicing and modeling generosity in their own lives.

Each week they shared the truth of God's Word in a way that could be understood. They didn't compromise or bend the truth, but they were practical in their application.

Neither one was perfect. They were just men who genuinely loved God and wanted to do their best to serve Him and people. They shared that often through self-deprecating humor.

They were committed to quality and excellence, believing that you give God your best, not what's leftover.

Pastor Titus showed us what it meant to minister to men in prison.

Adessa was impressed by how Pastor Titus allowed his wife to flourish in all of her God-given talents. (A new concept for us.)

I was impressed that even though we lived far away and were not the most active or popular kids in the youth group, Pastor Bob gave us special attention—even taking me golfing.

In so many ways, these men modeled for us what it means to be a true ride or die man of God. Adessa wrote in one of her books that she doubts she would have been open to the idea of going into ministry without their influence on her life. Even today, we still model our ministry after what we learned in those teenage years.

Today, both of these men are still in full-time ministry. Even in his seventies and fighting Parkinson's disease, Pastor Titus still travels to speak, holds men's conferences, writes books, and teaches in a Bible College. I hope I still have their ride or die attitude when I am their age.

Even more, I hope that someday people will say about me what I can say about them: *"He taught me how to represent Jesus well. He showed me how to do Christianity and ministry right. He made a difference in my life."*

That's the legacy of a ride or die man of God.

Today's Scripture:

An elder must be blameless, faithful to his wife, a man whose children believe and are not open to the charge of being wild and disobedient.

Since an overseer manages God's household, he must be blameless —not overbearing, not quick-tempered, not given to drunkenness, not violent, not pursuing dishonest gain.

Rather, he must be hospitable, one who loves what is good, who is self-controlled, upright, holy and disciplined. He must hold firmly to the trustworthy message as it has been taught, so that he can encourage others by sound doctrine and refute those who oppose it. (Titus 1:6-9, NIV)

-Jamie Holden, Founder, Mantour Ministries

Monday

Luke 19-20 ☐   Psalm 108 ☐

Memory Verse: *The end of all things is near. Therefore be alert and of sober mind so that you may pray.* (1 Peter 4:7, NIV)

Tuesday

Luke 21-22 ☐   Proverbs 21:1-8 ☐

Memory Verse: *Above all, love each other deeply, because love covers over a multitude of sins.* (1 Peter 4:8, NIV)

Wednesday

Luke 23-24 ☐   Psalm 109 ☐

Memory Verse: *Offer hospitality to one another without grumbling.* (1 Peter 4:9, NIV)

Thursday

Genesis 1-2 ☐   Proverbs 21:9-19 ☐

Memory Verse: *Each of you should use whatever gift you have received to serve others, as faithful stewards of God's grace in its various forms.* (1 Peter 4:10, NIV)

Friday

Genesis 3-4 ☐   Psalm 110 ☐

Memory Verse: *If anyone speaks, they should do so as one who speaks the very words of God. If anyone serves, they should do so with the strength God provides, so that in all things God may be praised through Jesus Christ. To him be the glory and the power for ever and ever. Amen.* (1 Peter 4:11, NIV)

Saturday

Genesis 6-7 ☐   Psalm 111 ☐

Memory Verse: *Dear friends, do not be surprised at the fiery ordeal that has come on you to test you, as though something strange were happening to you.* (1 Peter 4:12, NIV)

-WEEK TWENTY-NINE-

THOMAS
BY JAMIE HOLDEN

Have you ever felt like someone judged you unfairly? Maybe they heard one or two things about you, and suddenly you earn the reputation that you couldn't shake? Perhaps it happened when you were a small child or in school, and then next thing you know, that's your label for life.

Sometimes I think this is what happened to Thomas. I'll be honest and admit that often I feel sorry for the guy because I think he got a bad rap. We all know the story of Thomas saying, *"I need to see it before I believe that Jesus is resurrected."* It's how he got the name *"Doubting Thomas."*

As we read the Gospels, we see that Thomas could be labeled a pessimist, a realist, a glass-half-empty kind of guy. But this doesn't tell the whole story of Thomas.

In a lesser recognized passage, we read that Thomas was also very loyal. Long before the crucifixion and resurrection, Thomas proves he was ride or die with Jesus even as the realist inside of Him knew death was a very real possibility.

Here's the story:

Lazarus was dead to begin with (a little Dicken's humor). Jesus had just told the disciples that He was going to Jerusalem to raise him from the dead. (They didn't get it at first, but they caught on eventually.) Here's the problem: the disciples knew that Jerusalem was dangerous for Jesus. The ruling religious elite hated him and were looking for a way to get rid of him.

Remember: Thomas doesn't sugarcoat things. He's a realist. He knows going to Jerusalem could turn out very badly—not just for Jesus but for him, too.

What does he say?

> *"Thomas, nicknamed the Twin, said to his fellow disciples, 'Let's go, too—and die with Jesus.'" (John 11:16, NLT)*

There's no doubt about it. Thomas knew that, no matter what happened, he would ride or die with Jesus. Even if things turned out badly, he would be loyal to the end.

Obviously, we know that Thomas didn't die that day. He went on to see Jesus die and be resurrected. Church tradition says that he became a missionary far outside the Roman Empire, even planting a church in India. Ultimately, he was martyred for following Jesus.

So did Thomas struggle with doubt? Yeah, a few times in his life. Still, what defines the legacy of his life is loyalty. He should be known as ride or die, Thomas.

Today's Scripture:

"Thomas, nicknamed the Twin, said to his fellow disciples, 'Let's go, too—and die with Jesus.'" (John 11:16, NLT)

-Jamie Holden, Founder, Mantour Ministries

Monday

Genesis 8-9 ☐   Psalm 112 ☐

Memory Verse: *But rejoice inasmuch as you participate in the sufferings of Christ, so that you may be overjoyed when his glory is revealed.* (1 Peter 4:13, NIV)

Tuesday

Genesis 11:1-8 ☐   Genesis 12-13 ☐   Proverbs 21:20-31 ☐

Memory Verse: *If you are insulted because of the name of Christ, you are blessed, for the Spirit of glory and of God rests on you.* (1 Peter 4:14, NIV)

Wednesday

Genesis 14-15 ☐   Psalm 113 ☐

Memory Verse: *If you suffer, it should not be as a murderer or thief or any other kind of criminal, or even as a meddler.* (1 Peter 4:15, NIV)

Thursday

Genesis 16-17 ☐   Proverbs 22:1-9 ☐

Memory Verse: *However, if you suffer as a Christian, do not be ashamed, but praise God that you bear that name. For it is time for judgment to begin with God's household; and if it begins with us, what will the outcome be for those who do not obey the gospel of God?* (1 Peter 4:16-17, NIV)

Friday

Genesis 18-19 ☐   Psalm 114 ☐

Memory Verse: *And, "If it is hard for the righteous to be saved what will become of the ungodly and the sinner?"* (1 Peter 4:18, NIV)

Saturday

Genesis 20-21 ☐   Psalm 115 ☐

Memory Verse: *So then, those who suffer according to God's will should commit themselves to their faithful Creator and continue to do good.* (1 Peter 4:19, NIV)

-WEEK THIRTY-

NEHEMIAH'S SECRET WEAPON
BY DAN COURTNEY

Imagine being moved by someone else's situation so much that you would do ANYTHING to fix it! This is the story of Nehemiah, who is best known for rebuilding the walls around Jerusalem. Because of that accomplishment, the book of Nehemiah is seen as one of the best books to study on leadership.

The situation was bleak. After being overrun by the Babylonian army, the Jews were kicked out of Jerusalem. Most were either taken captive by the Babylonians or completely scattered around the known world. The walls of Jerusalem were broken down, and the gates burned. No one had lived there for seventy years. Now they were allowed to come back, but it was a mess. No protection, no pride; it was like living in the slums. And they were poor. They had nothing.

Nehemiah showed up to rebuild the city walls that were 2.5 miles around, nearly 40' tall, and over 8' wide. With God's favor, Israel regained its national pride, security, and restored worship and reading God's Word. Despite constant attacks from enemy nations, they rebuilt the entire wall in just 52 days. Here's some of how it happened...

First, God gave Nehemiah favor with King Artaxerxes to GIVE him all of the supplies he would need for the job. WHAT?!? Nehemiah was only a servant for the king. In fact, his whole job was to make sure the king's drinks were the way he liked them, three creams & one sugar, and to keep him from getting poisoned. He was a nobody...but God gave him favor.

Free supplies are amazing, but the real leadership was how he got the people to believe in a vision and work together. These were a defeated people with no desire to work. God gave him an amazing plan of having every family work on the part of the wall that would be closest to their home. If they wanted protection for their family, they had to build it. And they did!

One of my favorite stories in Nehemiah was after serious threats from enemy armies. Their response is incredible, *"...The laborers carried on their work with one hand supporting their load and one hand holding a weapon." (Nehemiah 4:17, NLT)* No enemy was going to stop them. They even worked while holding a weapon, ready to fight! God gave them favor over their enemies several times.

Throughout the progression of his story, you'll see: Nehemiah had favor with the King, defeated enemies without a real army, dealt with internal problems, built a wall, and restored worship! In the end, he also held people accountable to God's ways...even to the extreme of *"kicking them and pulling out their hair!"* (You have to read the book to see this part...it's in there!)

But HOW? How did this nobody get so much favor? One word, PRAYER. Seriously. The entire secret of Nehemiah can be summed up in Nehemiah 1:4 (NLT), which takes place right after he learned of the dire state Jerusalem was in, *"When I heard this, I sat down and wept. In fact, for days I mourned, fasted, and prayed to the God of heaven."*

If you study this book, you will find that BEFORE Nehemiah ever did anything, he prayed. Prayer was his FIRST resort, and he is one of the most powerful leaders in the entire Bible.

I think Nehemiah understood that prayer was not simply talking TO God. To him, it was a time of connecting with God's heart, learning from Him what direction to take, and acknowledging that

God could accomplish things that he could never achieve on his own.

What about you? Do you desire to accomplish great things? Do you want to be a good and strong man, leader, husband, brother, dad? How is your prayer life? Do you tend to pray only when everything else fails? Perhaps it's time to take a page from Nehemiah...and pray FIRST before you take action. Also, try talking less and listening more as you pray.

Here's the challenge: What would it look like to start your day with prayer? How could you be more intentional about praying before you take action?

Today's Scripture:

When I heard this, I sat down and wept. In fact, for days I mourned, fasted, and prayed to the God of heaven. (Nehemiah 1:4, NLT)

-Dan Courtney, Pastor,
https://www.youtube.com/c/DevotionswithDan

Monday

Genesis 22-23 ☐   Psalm 116 ☐

Memory Verse: *To the elders among you, I appeal as a fellow elder and a witness of Christ's sufferings who also will share in the glory to be revealed:* (1 Peter 5:1, NIV)

Tuesday

Genesis 24-25 ☐   Proverbs 22:10-16 ☐

Memory Verse: *Be shepherds of God's flock that is under your care, watching over them—not because you must, but because you are willing, as God wants you to be; not pursuing dishonest gain, but eager to serve;* (1 Peter 5:2, NIV)

Wednesday

Genesis 26-27 ☐   Psalm 117 ☐

Memory Verse: *Not lording it over those entrusted to you, but being examples to the flock.* (1 Peter 5:3, NIV)

Thursday

Genesis 28-29 ☐   Proverbs 22:17-21 ☐

Memory Verse: *And when the Chief Shepherd appears, you will receive the crown of glory that will never fade away.* (1 Peter 5:4, NIV)

Friday

Genesis 30-31 ☐   Psalm 118 ☐

Memory Verse: *In the same way, you who are younger, submit yourselves to your elders. All of you, clothe yourselves with humility toward one another, because, "God opposes the proud but shows favor to the humble."* (1 Peter 5:5, NIV)

Saturday

Genesis 32-33 ☐   Psalm 119:1-8 ☐

Memory Verse: *Humble yourselves, therefore, under God's mighty hand, that he may lift you up in due time.* (1 Peter 5:6, NIV)

-WEEK THIRTY-ONE-

DAVID: AN IMPERFECT RIDE OR DIE MAN OF GOD
BY ROLAND COON

David was a man that God called *"a man after His own heart."* This was quite special, even though David would be a man who would fall into temptation and commit adultery.

God knew David would do that, yet, He kept David in kingship because of a promise to Israel and his repentance (Psalm 51). It was not without hardship in his family from that point on, but David stayed the course.

He stayed on the ride God laid out for him. While a great warrior, David was also tender-hearted and compassionate. I believe one reason he was this way was that he knew that he had failed morally, so how could he be hard and harsh on others?

There are a few lessons we need to think about on our journey with God:

First, we are not perfect, yet when we hear bad news, we can be judgmental and throw out our opinions. Be careful here as someone could easily do that about us. That's not suggesting that we have a long list of issues, but we must remember that we are imperfect, and we can fall as quickly as someone else if we are not careful.

When I was interviewing for the church in Dover, Delaware, where I spent forty years as a pastor, there was a discussion going on with the board members that evening around the table. During the discussion, one of the board members said he would be in Chicago

on training for his job at the Dover Air Force Base. One of the other board members said to him, *"I do not think I could go and be without my wife and not be tempted by other women."*

I was surprised to hear that coming from a board member where I may serve as a pastor! The board member who was going on the trip said something that stuck with me throughout my ministry in Dover, Delaware. He said, *"I would hope that I would not make the wrong decision."*

Wow!! What a powerful response. He was not saying he would never do it, but that he was going on this trip with a determination not to be unfaithful to his wife. He knew he was human and not perfect, but at the same time, abundantly clear that as men of God, on this ride in life, we have to choose to make the right choices. That's our part, and God does the rest. Guess who became my accountability partner for many years before he went home to be with his wife in heaven? He did. His name was Harold Hall.

Second, find someone who can ride along with you in life to bear your soul if need be. If you are married, your wife can be very supportive, but you need another man in your life. They need you, too.

Finally, stay humble and listen well to others. It was hard on David with some of his family members working against him, but he listened to his advisers. In the multitude of counsel, there is safety.

David made it to the end of the ride God laid out to him. We can do the same thing by keeping in mind that we are not perfect. We stay ahead of temptation by choosing as soon as we leave the house each day to concentrate on making wise decisions. At the same time, have an accountability partner and stay humble.

Enjoy the ride. You have God on your side.

Today's Scripture:

Watch and pray so that you will not fall into temptation. The spirit is willing, but the flesh is weak. (Matthew 26:41, NIV)

-Pastor Roland Coon, Retired Pastor and Presbyter, 4One Ministries Board of Directors

Monday

Genesis 34-35 ☐   Psalm 119:9-16 ☐

Memory Verse: *Cast all your anxiety on him because he cares for you.* (1 Peter 5:7, NIV)

Tuesday

Genesis 37-38 ☐   Proverbs 22:22-23 ☐

Memory Verse: *Be alert and of sober mind. Your enemy the devil prowls around like a roaring lion looking for someone to devour.* (1 Peter 5:8, NIV)

Wednesday

Genesis 39-40 ☐   Psalm 119:17-24 ☐

Memory Verse: *Resist him, standing firm in the faith, because you know that the family of believers throughout the world is undergoing the same kind of sufferings.* (1 Peter 5:9, NIV)

Thursday

Genesis 41-42 ☐   Proverbs 22:24-25 ☐

Memory Verse: *And the God of all grace, who called you to his eternal glory in Christ, after you have suffered a little while, will himself restore you and make you strong, firm and steadfast.* (1 Peter 5:10, NIV)

Friday

Genesis 43-44 ☐   Psalm 119:25-32 ☐

Memory Verse: *To him be the power for ever and ever. Amen.*
(1 Peter 5:11, NIV)

Saturday

Genesis 45-46:1-7 ☐   Genesis 46:26-31☐   Psalm 119:33-40 ☐

Memory Verse: *Greet one another with a kiss of love. Peace to all of you who are in Christ.* (1 Peter 5:14, NIV)

THOUGHTS AND REFLECTIONS

WEEK THIRTY-TWO

THE STORY OF AITEY
BY DUANE GOODLING

In March 2018, I co-led a mission team to India to begin a Bible school building project. During our free day, we visited a Buddhist temple in the small mountain village of Lava, near India's border with Bhutan. As we approached Lava and before we went to the temple, we visited the home of a man named Aitey (pronounced *'eye-tee'*).

From a very young age, Aitey was destined to high priesthood in the Buddhist temple, and over time, he rose in their leadership ranks. As an adult, Aitey was president of over 55 Buddhist houses and was a very respected leader in and around Lava. It was then that he started having problems with his throat. None of the area doctors could figure it out. He experienced a lot of pain, fatigue, and had difficulty speaking, often completely losing his voice.

Aitey tried Buddhist priests, Muslim clerics, witchcraft, and other healers, but no one could treat his issues. The constant pain was so bad that he began drinking alcohol to dull it and got to the point where he just wanted to die. He was suffering so much that he paid up all of his insurance and decided he would commit suicide by crashing his car so his family could be taken care of after his death. Aitey's sister, who lived with him, secretly started attending a Christian church during this time. However, when Aitey found out, he kicked her out of his home.

Four to five days before he planned to kill himself, his sister called and said he tried everything else. Why doesn't he go to the Christian church and ask the pastor to pray for him? But, Aitey's pride would not allow him to do this. However, the day before he planned to kill himself, when he felt he had no other options but death, he decided to go to the Christian pastor; but only at night so he wouldn't be seen. After all, a highly-respected Buddhist priest could never be seen visiting a Christian pastor.

This pastor told him that God could heal him. Aitey said he would accept Jesus if he is healed, and he prayed four times, but nothing happened. The pastor told him that if he wanted to be healed, he must accept Jesus first. Aitey was at rock bottom and had no other options left except death, so he finally relented and accepted Jesus as Lord and Savior.

Immediately afterward, he started coughing. He coughed up a lump of dark-colored, foul-smelling substance. The pain began to subside, his voice started to return, and he returned to full strength over approximately the next four months.

It was about five to six years later when we met him, and he is completely healed. He now uses the Christian name Joshua, writes and sings songs, and is an elder in a Christian church in the same village of Lava where he was a Buddhist priest.

We face many adversities in this life, and we often try to face them alone or try worldly means to resolve them. This is what Aitey did; when faced with a severe physical ailment, he tried other religions, he tried witchcraft, and when none of those worked, he was going to take it into his own hands and kill himself. Thank God for someone like his sister who told Aitey that there was Someone Who could heal him.

She wasn't raised in the church. She was only a Christian for a short time, and she had just been thrown out of her brothers' home, but she still had the faith and courage to tell him the truth. This was a huge risk for her, but she did it.

As for Aitey, even after hearing the truth, he still had to take what he heard and trust that it was indeed true. He was a Buddhist priest in leadership in the temple; he had to risk everything to accept Christ, but he did and received healing for his act of faith. He faced persecution from the monks at the temple in Lava, but this did not stop him from preaching the Word. His testimony has led many people to accept Christ in and around Lava.

What challenges do you face that you have not yet turned over to the Lord? Or maybe someone you know needs to hear the truth. What are you waiting for?

Today's Scripture:

Then I heard the voice of the Lord saying, "Whom shall I send? And who will go for us?"

And I said, "Here am I. Send me!" (Isaiah 6:8, NIV)

-Duane Goodling, Mission Director- Think Missions, www.thinkmissions.org

Monday

Genesis 47-48 □   Psalm 119:41-48 □

Memory Verse: *Simon Peter, a servant and apostle of Jesus Christ, to those who through the righteousness of our God and Savior Jesus Christ have received a faith as precious as ours.   Grace and peace be yours in abundance through the knowledge of God and of Jesus our Lord.*
(2 Peter 1:1-2, NIV)

Tuesday

Genesis 49-50 □   Proverbs 22:26-27 □

Memory Verse: *His divine power has given us everything we need for a godly life through our knowledge of him who called us by his own glory and goodness.* (2 Peter 1:3, NIV)

Wednesday

1 Peter 1-2 □   Psalm 119:49-56 □

Memory Verse: *Through these he has given us his very great and precious promises, so that through them you may participate in the divine nature, having escaped the corruption in the world caused by evil desires.*
(2 Peter 1:4, NIV)

Thursday

1 Peter 3-4 □   Proverbs 22:28-29 □

Memory Verse: *For this very reason, make every effort to add to your faith goodness; and to goodness, knowledge; and to knowledge, self-control; and to self-control, perseverance; and to perseverance, godliness; and to godliness, mutual affection; and to mutual affection, love.* (2 Peter 1:5-7, NIV)

Friday

1 Peter 5 □   2 Peter 1 □   Psalm 119:57-64 □

Memory Verse: *For if you possess these qualities in increasing measure, they will keep you from being ineffective and unproductive in your knowledge of our Lord Jesus Christ.* (2 Peter 1:8, NIV)

Saturday

2 Peter 2-3 □   Psalm 119:65-72 □

Memory Verse: *But whoever does not have them is nearsighted and blind, forgetting that they have been cleansed from their past sins.* (2 Peter 1:9, NIV)

-Week Thirty-Three-

PAUL
BY JAMIE HOLDEN

Rejoice in the Lord always. I will say it again: Rejoice!
(Philippians 4:4, NIV)

I know what it is to be in need, and I know what it is to have
plenty. I have learned the secret of being content in any and every
situation, whether well fed or hungry, whether living in plenty or
in want. I can do all this through him who gives me strength.
(Philippians 4:12-13, NIV)

Have you ever stopped and considered that these popular Scriptures were written from a jail cell? Yes, the entire book of Philippians, often referred to as *"the book on joy,"* was written from a common cell in a Roman jail.

Yet, even in this dark, difficult place, Paul still had a ride or die attitude. *"Whatever I face, I'm all in for Jesus!"* That was Paul's life motto.

Let's be honest: Paul faced some pretty difficult things. Let's hear about it in his own words:

> *I have worked much harder, been in prison more*
> *frequently, been flogged more severely, and been*
> *exposed to death again and again. Five times I*
> *received from the Jews the forty lashes minus one.*
> *Three times I was beaten with rods, once I was pelted*
> *with stones, three times I was shipwrecked, I spent a*

night and a day in the open sea, I have been constantly on the move.

I have been in danger from rivers, in danger from bandits, in danger from my fellow Jews, in danger from Gentiles; in danger in the city, in danger in the country, in danger at sea; and in danger from false believers. I have labored and toiled and have often gone without sleep; I have known hunger and thirst and have often gone without food; I have been cold and naked. (2 Cor 11:23-27, NIV)

Yet, through it all, Paul's attitude and motivation never changed… his mission was to ride or die for Jesus and to spread the Gospel.

In these attitudes, Paul sets an example that we can all follow. Let's be real…we all go through difficult times. As ride or die men who are fully committed to God, this is to be expected. As Paul told Timothy in 2 Timothy 3:12: *"Everyone who wants to live a godly life in Christ Jesus will be persecuted."* (NIV)

We see this every day as men who are committed to following God's ways are slandered, ridiculed, and demonized. While most of us in America have yet to experience physical persecution, the day is quickly approaching when we may have to face loss of finances, loss of jobs, or loss of our personal freedom to follow Christ. Whatever the cost, as men who choose to ride or die for God in an ungodly culture, we can expect to suffer and be persecuted.

We follow Paul's example when we see it as an opportunity to suffer for Christ and continue to *"rejoice because great is our reward in Heaven."* (Matthew 5:12)

Paul reminds all of us that Christians are never promised a cushy, comfortable, name-it-and-claim-it life. That's not Biblical. Instead, we are given the privilege of suffering for the sake of the Gospel and rejoicing while we do it.

Whether we ride or whether we die, we are totally committed to following Jesus!

Today's Scripture:

Blessed are you when people insult you, persecute you and falsely say all kinds of evil against you because of me. Rejoice and be glad, because great is your reward in heaven, for in the same way they persecuted the prophets who were before you.
(Matthew 5:11-12, NIV)

-Jamie Holden, Founder, Mantour Ministries

Monday

Exodus 1-2 ☐   Psalm 119:73-80 ☐

Memory Verse: *Therefore, my brothers and sisters, make every effort to confirm your calling and election. For if you do these things, you will never stumble, and you will receive a rich welcome into the eternal kingdom of our Lord and Savior Jesus Christ.*(2 Peter 1:10-11, NIV)

Tuesday

Exodus 3-4 ☐   Proverbs 23:1-3 ☐

Memory Verse: *So I will always remind you of these things, even though you know them and are firmly established in the truth you now have.* (2 Peter 1:12, NIV)

Wednesday

Exodus 5 ☐   Exodus 6:1-12 ☐   Exodus 6:38-30 ☐
Psalm 119:81-88 ☐

Memory Verse: *I think it is right to refresh your memory as long as I live in the tent of this body, because I know that I will soon put it aside, as our Lord Jesus Christ has made clear to me.* (2 Peter 1:13-14, NIV)

Thursday

Exodus 7-8 ☐   Proverbs 23:4-5 ☐

Memory Verse: *And I will make every effort to see that after my departure you will always be able to remember these things.* (2 Peter 1:15, NIV)

Friday

Exodus 9-10☐   Psalm 119:89-96 ☐

Memory Verse: *For we did not follow cleverly devised stories when we told you about the coming of our Lord Jesus Christ in power, but we were eyewitnesses of his majesty.* (2 Peter 1:16, NIV)

Saturday

Exodus 11-12 ☐   Psalm 119:97-104 ☐

Memory Verse: *He received honor and glory from God the Father when the voice came to him from the Majestic Glory, saying, "This is my Son, whom I love; with him I am well pleased." We ourselves heard this voice that came from heaven when we were with him on the sacred mountain.* (2 Peter 1:17-18, NIV)

-WEEK THIRTY-FOUR-

THE "NO NAME" FRIENDS
BY ERIC SPANIER

There are so many great examples of great men throughout Scripture (and even throughout history) who did great things for God. I'm sure most men could rattle off a few of these men by name without even giving it much thought. Why? Because their NAME is synonymous with what they have done. When we hear their NAME, we can immediately recall what they have done and the wonderful impact they have made in the world around them.

In Luke chapter 5, we read about an encounter that a paralyzed man had with Jesus. In this encounter, Jesus is teaching at someone's house, and a large crowd begins to form inside and outside the home. The people from the town are there, the disciples are there, and we also learn that some religious leaders are there.

It would seem almost impossible for someone who is paralyzed to be able to get close enough to Jesus and hear His powerful teaching – and maybe even experience His healing power. This is where the encounter takes a wonderful turn: ***"Some men came carrying a paralytic on a mat and tried to take him into the house to lay him before Jesus. When they could not find a way to do this because of the crowd, they went up on the roof and lowered him on his mat through the tiles into the middle of the crowd, right in front of Jesus." (Luke 5:18-19, NIV)***

Did you catch what's happening? Are you sure? Most of the time, when we read a passage like this, we focus on the paralyzed man whose life is about to change. We are on the edge of our seats, wondering what will happen next. Will Jesus stop teaching? Will Jesus even notice the man? Will Jesus heal the paralyzed man? We are completely focused on the MAIN CHARACTER – that we easily forget about the *"NO NAME"* friends.

For these *"NO NAME"* friends, it wasn't enough to get their paralyzed friend to the outskirts of the crowd so that he could faintly hear Jesus' teaching. For these *"NO NAME"* friends, it wasn't enough to get their paralyzed friend around other sick people who may have been waiting at the possibility of getting healed. For these *"NO NAME"* friends, it was all about getting their friend into the presence of Jesus because they knew that it was in the presence of Jesus where his life could change. They were willing to do whatever was necessary to make this happen – even to go as far as to carry their friend to the roof, rip the shingles off the roof, make a hole in the roof, develop some sort of pulley system, and then lower their friend through the roof directly into the presence of Jesus.

Their FAITH in Jesus affected everything that was about to happen for their friend. Watch what happens next: **"When Jesus saw their faith, He said, 'Friend, your sins are forgiven.' ... (Jesus) said to the paralyzed man, 'I tell you, get up, take your mat and go home.' Immediately he stood up in front of them, took what he had been lying on and went home praising God." (Luke 5:20, 24-25, NIV)**

Did you notice what happened? It wasn't the faith of the paralyzed man that impressed Jesus; rather, it was the faith of these *"NO NAME"* friends. Jesus responded to their faith and healed their friend.

THE CHALLENGE: Are we OK with being the *"NO NAME"* friend who does the hard work of getting other people to Jesus so that He can change them, forgive them, and heal them?

As a man in our culture, it seems to be so important to *"make a name for ourselves."* We want to do something so significant and so earth-shattering that other people will remember our NAME. Do you know what's so amazing? You are reading this devotional that references something amazing that happened over 2,000 years ago, and we still don't know their NAMES. But, we know the impact that their faith made on their friend, on the crowd, and on everyone who would read about it.

Our FAITH affects OTHERS – whether people know our names or not. Are we OK with being the *"NO NAME"* friend who does the hard work of getting other people to Jesus so that He can change them, forgive them, and heal them?

Today's Scripture:

Some men came carrying a paralyzed man on a mat and tried to take him into the house to lay him before Jesus. When they could not find a way to do this because of the crowd, they went up on the roof and lowered him on his mat through the tiles into the middle of the crowd, right in front of Jesus. When Jesus saw their faith, he said, "Friend, your sins are forgiven." (Luke 5:18-20, NIV)

-Eric Spanier, Pastor, New City Church, Wilmington, DE

Monday

Exodus 13-14 ☐   Psalm 119:105-112 ☐

Memory Verse: *We also have the prophetic message as something completely reliable, and you will do well to pay attention to it, as to a light shining in a dark place, until the day dawns and the morning star rises in your hearts.* (2 Peter 1:19, NIV)

Tuesday

Exodus 15-16 ☐   Proverbs 23:6-9 ☐

Memory Verse: *Above all, you must understand that no prophecy of Scripture came about by the prophet's own interpretation of things.* (2 Peter 1:20, NIV)

Wednesday

Exodus 17-18 ☐   Psalm 119:113-120 ☐

Memory Verse: *For prophecy never had its origin in the human will, but prophets, though human, spoke from God as they were carried along by the Holy Spirit.* (2 Peter 1:21, NIV)

Thursday

Exodus 19-20 ☐   Proverbs 23:10-12 ☐

Memory Verse: *But there were also false prophets among the people, just as there will be false teachers among you. They will secretly introduce destructive heresies, even denying the sovereign Lord who bought them—bringing swift destruction on themselves.* (2 Peter 2:1, NIV)

Friday

Exodus 24 ☐   Exodus 29 ☐   Psalm 119:121-128 ☐

Memory Verse: *Many will follow their depraved conduct and will bring the way of truth into disrepute.* (2 Peter 2:2, NIV)

Saturday

Exodus 31-32 ☐   Psalm 119:129-136 ☐

Memory Verse: *In their greed these teachers will exploit you with fabricated stories. Their condemnation has long been hanging over them, and their destruction has not been sleeping.* (2 Peter 2:3, NIV)

THOUGHTS AND REFLECTIONS

WEEK THIRTY-FIVE

JIM ELLIOT
BY JAMIE HOLDEN

In elementary school, I first read *"Through Gates of Splendor,"* the story of Jim Elliot. In our small Christian school, it was required reading. Like me, Jim was raised in a Christian home and felt God's call to ministry early in his life. Very successful and skilled in many areas, family and friends encouraged Jim to be a youth pastor stateside. However, it broke his heart that so many people throughout the world had never heard about Jesus. This created a passion inside of Jim for foreign missions.

Jim attended Wheaton College, and then at the age of 23, he started training to be a missionary at Camp Wycliffe. There he began language studies with a former missionary to the Quechua people. This missionary first told him about the Auca Indians—an unfriendly, violent, murderous people in Ecuador known to hate outsiders. This planted the seed in Jim's heart to reach these people for Jesus— but it wasn't quite time yet.

In February of 1952, Jim Elliot and Nate Flemming went to Ecuador to replace a retiring missionary. They learned the language and ministered to the people in the jungle. A year later, Jim married Elizabeth, and she joined him on the mission field. They ministered to the Quechua Indians for three years before they felt God's call to reach the Auca Indians he'd heard about years before.

Knowing the unfriendly and violent reputation of the Aucas, Jim and his team knew they couldn't just show up in their village.

Creatively, they used the resources they had. Nate Saint was a pilot, and he configured a way to lower a basket of gifts from the plane. They did this for several months, giving gifts and using an amplifier to call out friendly phrases to let the Aucas know they came in a spirit of friendship. When the Aucas sent a gift back up in the basket, Jim and his team knew it was time to make contact.

They built their first attempt at contact on their use of the plane. Four of the missionaries went to the beach while the pilot, Nate Saint, flew over the village inviting the people to come out and meet them. A tiny group went to the beach, where they shared a meal with the missionaries, and Nate even took one for a ride in their plane. It looked like a breakthrough, and the missionaries encouraged their new friends to bring others with them next time.

They did. Only it wasn't for the reasons the missionaries planned.

On January 8, 1956, Jim Elliot, Roger Youderian, Nate Sait, Ed McCully, and Pete Fleming were waiting on the beach when they saw a small group approach. Believing they came in friendship, they radioed their wives asking for prayer and promising to call when their meeting was over. The call never came.

Instead of coming in peace, the few people in front were a ruse for those who would attack and slaughter the five missionaries. Even though the missionaries had guns and shot a few rounds into the air, they had made a pact beforehand that they would not kill anyone who did not know Jesus. They didn't want to be responsible for sending anyone to Hell.

That day, all five missionaries died on the beach. But their legacy lives on.

Just under two years later, Jim's wife, Elizabeth, and their daughter, Valerie, went with Nate Saint's sister to continue the ministry to the Auca Indians. Because the Indians were so impressed that the missionaries didn't fight back and that these women could forgive them and still wanted to minister to them, many Indians became Christians. Work among this tribe continues today because of the ride or die attitude of five men who would do anything to reach people for the Gospel.

Their testimony doesn't end there. Through Jim's wife's books and a movie about his life, many more people were challenged to go into foreign missions work. Even though I'm not a foreign missionary, throughout my life, I have been inspired and encouraged by Jim's quote, *"He is no fool who gives what he cannot keep to gain that which he cannot lose."*

Many times I've thought of these words when the Holy Spirit has been challenging me to take a step of faith and follow Him ride or die.

Today their testimony challenges all of us to follow God's call on our lives even when it seems foolish or even dangerous. Their story challenges us that seeing people spend eternity with Jesus is more important than self-preservation here on earth. They truly had a ride or die attitude. In life and death, they were totally committed to Jesus.

They inspire us to do the same.

Today's Scripture:

For whoever wants to save their life will lose it, but whoever loses their life for me will save it. What good is it for someone to gain the whole world, and yet lose or forfeit their very self? (Luke 9:24-25, NIV)

-Jamie Holden, Founder, Mantour Ministries

Monday

1 John 1-2 ☐   Proverbs 23:13-18 ☐

Memory Verse: *For if God did not spare angels when they sinned, but sent them to hell, putting them in chains of darkness to be held for judgment;* (2 Peter 2:4, NIV)

Tuesday

1 John 3-4 ☐   Psalm 119:145-152 ☐

Memory Verse: *If he did not spare the ancient world when he brought the flood on its ungodly people, but protected Noah, a preacher of righteousness, and seven others;* (2 Peter 2:5, NIV)

Wednesday

1 John 5 ☐   2 John ☐   Proverbs 23:19-25 ☐

Memory Verse: *If he condemned the cities of Sodom and Gomorrah by burning them to ashes, and made them an example of what is going to happen to the ungodly;* (2 Peter 2:6, NIV)

Thursday

3 John ☐   Jude ☐   Psalm 119:153-160 ☐

Memory Verse: *And if he rescued Lot, a righteous man, who was distressed by the depraved conduct of the lawless (for that righteous man, living among them day after day, was tormented in his righteous soul by the lawless deeds he saw and heard)* (2 Peter 2:6-8, NIV)

Friday

Numbers 9 ☐   Psalm 119:161-164 ☐

Memory Verse: *If this is so, then the Lord knows how to rescue the godly from trials and to hold the unrighteous for punishment on the day of judgment.* (2 Peter 2:9, NIV)

Saturday

Numbers 10 ☐   Psalm 119:165-168 ☐

Memory Verse: *This is especially true of those who follow the corrupt desire of the flesh and despise authority.* (2 Peter 2:10a, NIV)

-WEEK THIRTY-SIX-

JOSHUA
BY JAMIE HOLDEN

One of my favorite guys in the Bible has always been Joshua. He was truly one of the greats!! Someday, I'm going to write a book about him.

Yet, one thing that's important to remember about Joshua is that he didn't become one of the most incredible men in the Bible overnight. Long before God told him to be *"strong and courageous,"* decades before the walls of Jericho fell, or he led the children of Israel to finally enter the Promised Land, Joshua was ride or die for God. His story doesn't start in the book that carries his name. Instead, it begins in Exodus.

In Exodus, we see that Joshua's first title wasn't *"leader."* It was *"Moses' aide."* ***"Then Moses set out with Joshua his aide" (Exodus 24:13, NIV)***

Numbers 11:28 tells us that Joshua was Moses' aide since his youth. Basically, he was Moses' assistant. Where Moses went, he went. When Moses needed help, he was the one who gave it.

Even when Moses went to Mt. Sinai, Joshua was there. (Exodus 24:13)

When they came down from the mountain, and the people had built the golden calf, Joshua was with Moses. (Joshua 32:17)

In Exodus 17:8-16, Joshua led the Israelites in battle under the direction of Moses.

Exodus 33:7-11 tells us that Joshua even went with Moses to

meet God in the Tent of Meeting.

Numbers 13 shows us that Joshua was one of the twelve men sent to spy out the Promised Land. He was one of only two who said, *"Let's do it, ride or die."* When the people refused, Joshua continued serving as Moses' aid for the next forty years.

The amazing thing about Joshua is that he didn't see his time as an *"aide"* as a waste. Instead, with a ride or die attitude toward God and Moses, he took full advantage of the opportunity. He learned from every experience. Exodus 33:11 tells us that he lingered in the presence of God—developing his own deep, personal relationship.

He wasn't just filling time—he was allowing God to prepare him for the day when he would graduate from Moses' aide to Moses' successor.

In this area, we can all learn from Joshua. Too often, we fall into the trap of waiting for the *"big promotion,"* the title, the prestige. We feel like we are just filling time until we get our shot.

Yet, a true ride or die man of God serves faithfully at every level and in every circumstance.

We serve loyally. We are trustworthy. We are diligent and learn all we can from every situation. Most of all, we don't rely on others for our relationship with God, but we are constantly developing and strengthening our spiritual lives.

Whether we are the *"aide"* or the *"leader,"* we are wholeheartedly committed to fulfilling God's purpose for our lives—ride or die.

Today's Scripture:

The Lord would speak to Moses face to face, as one speaks to a friend. Then Moses would return to the camp, but his young aide Joshua son of Nun did not leave the tent. (Exodus 33:11, NIV)

-Jamie Holden, Founder, Mantour Ministries

Monday

Numbers 11-12 ☐   Psalm 119:169-176 ☐

Memory Verse: *Bold and arrogant, they are not afraid to heap abuse on celestial beings;* (2 Peter 2:10b, NIV)

Tuesday

Numbers 13-14☐   Proverbs 23:26-28 ☐

Memory Verse: *Yet even angels, although they are stronger and more powerful, do not heap abuse on such beings when bringing judgment on them from the Lord.* (2 Peter 2:11, NIV)

Wednesday

Numbers 16-17☐   Psalm 120 ☐

Memory Verse: *But these people blaspheme in matters they do not understand. They are like unreasoning animals, creatures of instinct, born only to be caught and destroyed, and like animals they too will perish.* (2 Peter 2:12, NIV)

Thursday

Numbers 20-21☐   Proverbs 23:29-35 ☐

Memory Verse: *They will be paid back with harm for the harm they have done. Their idea of pleasure is to carouse in broad daylight. They are blots and blemishes, reveling in their pleasures while they feast with you.* (2 Peter 2:13, NIV)

Friday

Numbers 22-24☐   Psalm 121 ☐

Memory Verse: *With eyes full of adultery, they never stop sinning; they seduce the unstable; they are experts in greed—an accursed brood! They have left the straight way and wandered off to follow the way of Balaam son of Bezer, who loved the wages of wickedness. (2 Peter 2:14-15, NIV)*

Saturday

Numbers 25-27 ☐   Psalm 122 ☐

Memory Verse: *But he was rebuked for his wrongdoing by a donkey—an animal without speech—who spoke with a human voice and restrained the prophet's madness.* (2 Peter 2:16, NIV)

-WEEK THIRTY-SEVEN-

FIRST RESPONDERS
BY JAMIE HOLDEN

It was 9:00 a.m. September 11. 2001.

I flipped on the television to see the scores from the Broncos game the night before.

My Mom and sister were in the kitchen making my Dad a birthday cake.

Over the next few hours, we watched in horror as terrorists attacked our nation. First the Twin Towers, then the Pentagon, then Shanksville, Pa. As we watched and prayed from the safety of our home, others—men and women—were running toward the crash sites. They ran toward the falling buildings, toward the fire and smoke, toward the debris.

Firefighters. Police officers. Ambulance workers. EMTS. Chaplains. First Responders trained to respond to the worst-case scenario now raced an emergency no one ever imagined.

Not knowing if more attacks were coming....not knowing what they would find in the debris...with a ride or die attitude, they ran toward danger, trying to save as many lives as possible.

Over the next few days and weeks, even more would head into the wreckage, trying to save lives. When the rescue mission eventually became a recovery mission, they continued, trying to bring some comfort to the families who lost loved ones.

One of those men was my good friend, Tom Sember. A retired firefighter from Buffalo, New York, he went to Ground Zero in New York City to do all he could. His name, I know, but there are countless others whose names we don't know. Still, we cannot forget what they did that day.

The FBI states that more than 400 first responders, including 60 law enforcement officers, were killed on 9/11. Since then, many more have suffered life-changing illnesses from toxins they inhaled, helping others. Hundreds of New York City police officers and firefights have died since then from 9/11 related conditions, including cancers.

Why did they do it? Why did they run toward the danger when so many others were running away?

Could it be the same reason that the passangers of Flight 93 chose to take matters into their own hands and revolt against their captors? Deciding to take the plane from the hijackers before it could become a weapon against the White House or the Capitol, the passengers of Flight 93 lost their lives trying to save the lives of countless others. With the rallying cry of "*Let's Roll*," they exhibited ride or die courage until the last moment when their flight crashed in Shanksville, PA.

Since then, I've watched several documentaries that retold their story and reenacted their flights. Each time I've wondered what gave them the courage to choose the actions they did. Alongside, I've questioned if I'd have their same resolve.

One thing I know for sure: I am committed to never forgetting and always honoring the lives of the men and women who died that day. It's our duty as Americans to remember those who ran toward the building, those who stayed to clean up the mess, those who treated the wounded, and helped others escape.

That day, they showed us what it means to truly ride or die for our country, for our fellow man, and the brothers and sisters we work alongside. When they could have run away, they ran forward....helping the hurting without considering what agony it would cause them.

They are true heroes!

John 15:13 says, *"Greater love has no one than this: to lay down one's life for one's friends." (NIV)*

The first responders and passengers of Flight 9/11 embodied this verse that day.

They showed us what it means to give everything for the love of freedom, for the love of country, and the love of their fellowman.

Today, we honor their sacrifice and pray that we will have this same courage to ride or die for our faith, freedom, and those we love.

Never Forget!!

Today's Verse:

Greater love has no one than this: to lay down one's life for one's friends. (John 15:13, NIV)

-Jamie Holden, Founder, Mantour Ministries

Monday

Numbers 32 ☐   Numbers 35 ☐   Psalm 123 ☐

Memory Verse: *These people are springs without water and mists driven by a storm. Blackest darkness is reserved for them.* (2 Peter 2:17, NIV)

Tuesday

Numbers 36 ☐   Proverbs 24:1-7 ☐

Memory Verse: *For they mouth empty, boastful words and, by appealing to the lustful desires of the flesh, they entice people who are just escaping from those who live in error.* (2 Peter 2:18, NIV)

Wednesday

Hebrews 1-2 ☐   Psalm 124 ☐

Memory Verse: *They promise them freedom, while they themselves are slaves of depravity—for "people are slaves to whatever has mastered them."* (2 Peter 2:19, NIV)

Thursday

Hebrews 3-4 ☐   Proverbs 24:8-12 ☐

Memory Verse: *If they have escaped the corruption of the world by knowing our Lord and Savior Jesus Christ and are again entangled in it and are overcome, they are worse off at the end than they were at the beginning.* (2 Peter 2:20, NIV)

Friday

Hebrews 5-6 ☐   Psalm 125 ☐

Memory Verse: *It would have been better for them not to have known the way of righteousness, than to have known it and then to turn their backs on the sacred command that was passed on to them.* (2 Peter 2:21, NIV)

Saturday

Hebrews 7-8 ☐   Psalm 126 ☐

Memory Verse: *Of them the proverbs are true: "A dog returns to its vomit," and, "A sow that is washed returns to her wallowing in the mud."* (2 Peter 2:22, NIV)

-WEEK THIRTY-EIGHT-

JONATHAN AND DAVID: NO RIVALRY
BY SCOTT A. GRAY

Rivalry is found throughout the Bible. In fact, sibling rivalry extends nearly to the beginning of time that involved the first two brothers that the Bible mentions, Cain and Abel. The Merriam-Webster dictionary defines the noun *"rival"* as *"one of two or more striving to reach or obtain something that only one can possess; one striving for competitive advantage."* [1]

More than likely, in our personal lives, we can identify persons or groups of people that were our rivals either in school, in sports, at work, who perhaps exhibited common rival behaviors like *"trash talking."* Most of us would prefer cooperation over rivalry.

A story in the Bible found in 1 Samuel 18 involves King Saul, David, and Jonathan. There was a rivalry between King Saul and David, which was heightened by the action of women who came out from all the towns of Israel to meet King Saul and sang: *"Saul has slain his thousands, and David his tens of thousands" (1 Samuel 18:7, NIV).*

I can just imagine the jealousy and indignation surging up within King Saul. You probably felt that feeling, too. Someone else is receiving more accolades than you. Someone else is getting that promotion over you.

The Bible says in v. 8 that *"Saul was very angry."* He was so angry— to the point of trying to kill David with a spear the next day.

His anger eventually turned into hatred for David, and he feared his enemy because the Lord was with him. (1 Samuel 18:28-29, NIV)

King Saul wanted his oldest son Jonathan to kill David, but Jonathan denied his father's request. David and Jonathan should have been rivals, competing for the throne. However, Jonathan becomes David's ride or die kind of a friend.

What naturally should have been a competition resulted in a covenant between the two. The Bible says that *"After David had finished talking with Saul, Jonathan became one in spirit with David, and he loved him as himself...And Jonathan made a covenant with David because he loved him as himself."* (1 Samuel 18:1 & 3, NIV) Before these two men even exchanged words with each other, they loved each other in the sense of being like comrades on a battlefield, willing to lay down their lives for each other.

David was King Saul's ride or die, King Saul should have been David's ride or die, but Jonathan and David became ride or die friends. Jonathan proved it by giving David his robe he was wearing, along with his tunic, sword, bow, and belt! He literally gave his shirt off his back! Yet, this was more than mere generosity. This was humility from a true friend.

Jonathan was acknowledging David as the successor to his father's throne. One day he will be king of Israel. He thought more of his friend than he thought of himself. He forfeited kingship because he valued friendship.

That's the kind of friend that you need to be to the friends that God has placed in your life. Paul writes, *"Do nothing out of selfish ambition or vain conceit. Rather, in humility value others above yourselves, not looking to your own interests but each of you to the interests of the others." (Philippians 2:3-4, NIV)*

Let's get rid of our competitive spirit. Let's lay aside our envy or jealousy. Let's submit to the will of God and be a true friend who is willing to lay down our lives for others like Jonathan and Jesus ultimately did.

Today's Scripture:

"Do nothing out of selfish ambition or vain conceit. Rather, in humility value others above yourselves, not looking to your own interests but each of you to the interests of the others." (Philippians 2:3-4, NIV)

-Scott A. Gray, Associate Pastor, Lighthouse Church

Monday

Hebrews 9-10☐   Psalm 127 ☐

Memory Verse: *Dear friends, this is now my second letter to you. I have written both of them as reminders to stimulate you to wholesome thinking.* (2 Peter 3:1, NIV)

Tuesday

Hebrews 11-13☐   Proverbs 24:13-16 ☐

Memory Verse: *I want you to recall the words spoken in the past by the holy prophets and the command given by our Lord and Savior through your apostles.* (2 Peter 3:2, NIV)

Wednesday

Deuteronomy 31-22 ☐   Psalm 128 ☐

Memory Verse: *Above all, you must understand that in the last days scoffers will come, scoffing and following their own evil desires.* (2 Peter 3:3, NIV)

Thursday

Deuteronomy 33-34 ☐   Proverbs 24:17-22 ☐

Memory Verse: *They will say, "Where is this 'coming' he promised? Ever since our ancestors died, everything goes on as it has since the beginning of creation."* (2 Peter 3:4, NIV)

Friday

Isaiah 1-2☐   Psalm 129 ☐

Memory Verse: *But they deliberately forget that long ago by God's word the heavens came into being and the earth was formed out of water and by water.* (2 Peter 3:5, NIV)

Saturday

Isaiah 4:2-6 ☐   Isaiah 6-7 ☐   Psalm 130 ☐

Memory Verse: *By these waters also the world of that time was deluged and destroyed.* (2 Peter 3:6, NIV)

-WEEK THIRTY-NINE-

DIETRICK BONHOEFFER
BY KEN CLAFLIN

Dietrick Bonhoeffer was a German pastor who openly opposed the Nazi government during World War 2. He was arrested for taking part in an attempt to assassinate Adolf Hitler and was executed just before the end of the war.

Bonhoeffer was raised in the traditional Lutheran church, but experienced a personal revival as an adult. He became outspoken against compromise in the church. When the Nazi government began to deliberately influence church policy and practice, Bonhoeffer continued to be vocal about his objections.

In 1933, Bonhoeffer. was living in London and pastoring two German churches there. One of the reasons he had gone to London was to gain international support for his opposition to the Nazi influence over the German church. While in London, he wrote letters of opposition to national church leadership in Germany under which it continued to serve.

In a conversation with his German Bishop in London, Dietrick said the following:

"I mean that even in the evangelical Church we tend to think of Jesus' commands as historical artifacts, as sayings to be admired rather than obeyed without question. Most importantly, we fail to recognize them as commands at the precise moment at which the command is applicable. If we miss that moment, we've also missed our opportunity to

obey that command. It has become almost second nature for us as a Church to put things off, to study things to death, and then analyze the results of our indecision and disobedience. And all along we think that God is forgiving us. We are operating under a fallacy of cheap grace, thinking that we can bargain with God about our response." [1]

How long have you been a believer? Were you raised in church? Did you grow up going to Sunday school? Maybe you have only been a believer for a short while. If you have been a believer for any length of time, you have probably been taught that you should read the Bible daily. The combination of daily Bible reading and daily prayer is often referred to as *"having devotions"* or *"personal devotions."* It is one of the first things that we learn when we accept Christ as our personal Savior. These are both good things.

James urges us in James 1:22-25 (NIV):

> **"Do not merely listen to the word, and so deceive yourselves. Do what it says. Anyone who listens to the word but does not do what it says is like someone who looks at his face in a mirror and, after looking at himself, goes away and immediately forgets what he looks like. But whoever looks intently into the perfect law that gives freedom, and continues in it—not forgetting what they have heard, but doing it—they will be blessed in what they do."**

Dietrick accused believers of thinking of *"Jesus' commands as historical artifacts."* How often do we read right past the instruction of the Bible and don't take it to heart and don't put it into practice? It is well and good to read and study the Bible, but it is not beneficial unless we are DOING WHAT IT SAYS! When we read the Word, we should ask ourselves, *"What is God telling me to do?"* or *"How do I obey God in this area?"*.

Bonhoeffer personally applied the Scripture to his life as often as he could. He tried to live according to what the Scriptures teach. In the end, his uncompromising determination to be obedient to God in all things cost him his life.

Stop reading the Bible to simply learn what it says. As you read and as you study, be willing to live it, obey God, and put His Word into practice.

Today's Scripture:

Do not merely listen to the word, and so deceive yourselves. Do what it says. Anyone who listens to the word but does not do what it says is like someone who looks at his face in a mirror and, after looking at himself, goes away and immediately forgets what he looks like. But whoever looks intently into the perfect law that gives freedom, and continues in it—not forgetting what they have heard, but doing it—they will be blessed in what they do.
(James 1:22-25, NIV)

-Ken Claflin, Hamlin Assembly of God

Monday

Isaiah 11-12 ☐   Psalm 131 ☐

Memory Verse: By the same word the present heavens and earth are reserved for fire, being kept for the day of judgment and destruction of the ungodly. (2 Peter 3:7, NIV)

Tuesday

Isaiah 14 ☐   Isaiah 25 ☐   Proverbs 24:23-34 ☐

Memory Verse: *But do not forget this one thing, dear friends: With the Lord a day is like a thousand years, and a thousand years are like a day.* (2 Peter 3:8, NIV)

Wednesday

Isaiah 26-27 ☐   Psalm 132 ☐

Memory Verse: *The Lord is not slow in keeping his promise, as some understand slowness. Instead he is patient with you, not wanting anyone to perish, but everyone to come to repentance.* (2 Peter 3:9, NIV)

Thursday

Isaiah 32 ☐   Isaiah 35 ☐   Proverbs 25:1-10 ☐

Memory Verse: *But the day of the Lord will come like a thief. The heavens will disappear with a roar; the elements will be destroyed by fire, and the earth and everything done in it will be laid bare.* (2 Peter 3:10, NIV)

Friday

Isaiah 36-37 ☐   Psalm 133 ☐

Memory Verse: *Since everything will be destroyed in this way, what kind of people ought you to be? You ought to live holy and godly lives.* (2 Peter 3:11, NIV)

Saturday

Isaiah 38-39 ☐   Psalm 134 ☐

Memory Verse: *As you look forward to the day of God and speed its coming. That day will bring about the destruction of the heavens by fire, and the elements will melt in the heat.* (2 Peter 3:12, NIV)

-WEEK FORTY-

CALEB'S SECRET WEAPON
BY DAN COURTNEY

When I think about the great men of the Bible, Caleb is always one of the first that comes to mind. I think it is because I want my life to be like his in my later years. When the Israelite people had conquered the promised land and started dividing it up, Caleb stood tall at eighty-five years old and declared, *"I call the mountains...with the giants!!!"* Of course, those are my words, but that dude was hardcore!

What we read about in Joshua 14, actually started back under the leadership of Moses. Moses sent in twelve men to spy out the Promised Land. Caleb was one of them. They came back and reported on how amazing the land and its fruit were, but then ten of them went on and on about how powerful the people were that lived there and how big their city walls were. They even said, ***"Next to them we felt like grasshoppers."(Numbers 13:33b, NLT)*** In the midst of this bad report is when we see Caleb's secret weapon on full display.

Numbers 13:30 (NLT) says, ***"But Caleb tried to quiet the people as they stood before Moses. 'Let's go at once to take the land,' he said. 'We can certainly conquer it!'"***

As fear gripped everyone else, Caleb was bursting out of his skin to go and take the land. He wanted to go now! What was his secret weapon that allowed him to look past the fear and see the opportunity? It was FAITH. Not faith in himself, and not faith in a wandering community gripped by fear, but FAITH that God keeps His promises.

In Numbers 14, we see the people freaking out, even talking about getting a new leader and going back to Egypt. Along with Joshua (another spy), Caleb responded, *"The land we traveled through and explored is a wonderful land! And if the Lord is pleased with us, He will bring us safely into that land and give it to us. It is a rich land flowing with milk and honey. Do not rebel against the Lord, and don't be afraid of the people of the land. They are only helpless prey to us! They have no protection, but the Lord is with us! Don't be afraid of them!"* *(Numbers 14:7b-9, NLT)*

The people wouldn't listen to them and even wanted to kill Caleb and Joshua. When we trust in God as Caleb did, we don't always get to see the difference it makes, but Israel became divided into two very distinct destinies as a result of that conversation. God punished the Israelites severely for their lack of faith and trust in Him by sending them back into the wilderness until every unbelieving adult was dead.

As for Caleb, along with Joshua, they were in the wilderness, too. They didn't just survive the wilderness experience when all others died, but they also created a legacy for their families. The families of Caleb and Joshua were the only ones that had a true patriarch going into the Promised Land.

When you have faith, it affects more than just you. When you consider Caleb's story, faith was the difference between living out the rest of his life in a wilderness or getting to settle in the amazing land that God had promised him. The only bummer for Caleb is that he was an old man by the time he got HIS promised land. Or was it a bummer? Actually, it's a miracle that should drive us all the more to have FAITH in God.

In Joshua 14, Caleb explains how he was forty years old when he went in to spy out the land, and he gave an *"honest report,"* even though his brothers shared a frightening report and swayed the people. For his part, Moses promised him that the land he walked on would be his.

Then he says this, *"Now, as you can see, the Lord has kept me alive and well as he promised for all these forty-five years since Moses made this promise - even while Israel wandered in the wilderness. Today I am eighty-five years old. I am as strong now as I was when Moses sent me on that journey, and I can still travel and fight as well as I could then. So give me the hill country that the Lord promised me. (The giants live there...) But if the Lord is with me, I will drive them out of the land, just as the Lord said."* (*Joshua 14:10-12, NLT*)

Caleb's faith in God brought him through the wilderness and sustained him to be able to live out the promises of God that he had trusted all along. There is no evidence that his faith waned at all through the rough wilderness experience, and forty years is a long time! I'm sure he had some ups and downs, but Caleb was a man who truly trusted the Lord.

How about you, do you trust the Lord? When things are good? What about when times are challenging or downright brutal? In tough times, so many people abandon faith in God, but this is the time we actually need Him the most!

The key to building your faith is to make deposits every day by reading the Bible, praying, and putting other godly influences into your brain. If you keep making daily deposits, then you'll be able to have faith when you need it most!

Today's Scripture:

"Now, as you can see, the Lord has kept me alive and well as he promised for all these forty-five years since Moses made this promise - even while Israel wandered in the wilderness. Today I am eighty-five years old. I am as strong now as I was when Moses

sent me on that journey, and I can still travel and fight as well as I could then. So give me the hill country that the Lord promised me. (The giants live there...) But if the Lord is with me, I will drive them out of the land, just as the Lord said." (Joshua 14:10-12, NLT)

-Dan Courtney, Pastor
https://www.youtube.com/c/DevotionswithDan

Monday

Isaiah 40-41☐   Psalm 135 ☐

Memory Verse: *But in keeping with his promise we are looking forward to a new heaven and a new earth, where righteousness dwells.* (2 Peter 3:13, NIV)

Tuesday

Isaiah 42-43☐   Proverbs 25:11-20 ☐

Memory Verse: *So then, dear friends, since you are looking forward to this, make every effort to be found spotless, blameless and at peace with him.* (2 Peter 3:14, NIV)

Wednesday

Isaiah 44 ☐   Isaiah 49 ☐   Psalm 136 ☐

Memory Verse: *Bear in mind that our Lord's patience means salvation, just as our dear brother Paul also wrote you with the wisdom that God gave him.* (2 Peter 3:15, NIV)

Thursday

Isaiah 51-52 ☐   Proverbs 25:21-28 ☐

Memory Verse: *He writes the same way in all his letters, speaking in them of these matters. His letters contain some things that are hard to understand, which ignorant and unstable people distort, as they do the other Scriptures, to their own destruction.* (2 Peter 3:16, NIV)

Friday

Isaiah 53-54 ☐   Psalm 137 ☐

Memory Verse: *Therefore, dear friends, since you have been forewarned, be on your guard so that you may not be carried away by the error of the lawless and fall from your secure position.* (2 Peter 3:17, NIV)

Saturday

Isaiah 55-56 ☐   Psalm 138 ☐

Memory Verse: *But grow in the grace and knowledge of our Lord and Savior Jesus Christ. To him be glory both now and forever! Amen.* (2 Peter 3:18, NIV)

THOUGHTS AND

REFLECTIONS

-WEEK FORTY-ONE-

STEPHEN
BY JAMIE HOLDEN

One of the great questions of our time is, *"How can we follow Jesus' command to love our enemies while still speaking God's truth?"*

In the book of Acts, Stephen sets an example we can all follow when we are in this situation.

Let's take a look at his story:

> Stephen, a man full of God's grace and power, performed amazing miracles and signs among the people. But one day some men from the Synagogue of Freed Slaves, as it was called, started to debate with him. They were Jews from Cyrene, Alexandria, Cilicia, and the province of Asia. None of them could stand against the wisdom and the Spirit with which Stephen spoke.
>
> So they persuaded some men to lie about Stephen, saying, "We heard him blaspheme Moses, and even God." This roused the people, the elders, and the teachers of religious law. So they arrested Stephen and brought him before the high council.
>
> The lying witnesses said, "This man is always speaking against the holy Temple and against the law of Moses. We have heard him say that this Jesus of Nazareth will destroy the Temple and change the customs Moses

handed down to us." (Acts 6:8-14, NLT)

Even though he had done nothing wrong, Stephen was in deep trouble because of men who hated him, lied about him, and brought him before the courts.

Knowing he faced possible imprisonment or even death, Stephen had some choices to make.

He could back down and apologize for *"offending"* the Jews for his intolerance or the message that offended them and try to save his own skin. Or he could speak the truth and take the consequences.

This couldn't have been an easy decision, and yet, filled with the Holy Spirit, Stephen stood firm, spoke the truth, and preached the Gospel Message (including the parts they didn't want to hear) to the crowd.

If this were Hollywood, Stephen would have persuaded the people with his words, and there would have been a huge revival. That's not what happened. (Because the Bible is real.)

Instead, the Jewish leaders became enraged, dragged him out of the city, and stoned him.

This is where Stephen's ride or die character came shining through.

Instead of fighting them, responding in anger, or even calling down curses on them, Stephen followed Jesus' example and said, *"Lord, don't charge them with this sin!"*

And then he died.

In all of his actions, he set an example for us to follow.

You see, it's hard for us as Americans with our fight-to-win attitude to understand that as followers of Jesus, we are called to do both: stand for truth and love our enemies.

Like the people Jesus spoke to in Matthew 5:43-48, we see people as *'for us'* or *'against us,'* and we're tempted to love those who are for us while showing our angry, antagonistic side to those who disagree. Jesus said this is wrong. Instead, He said we should, *"Love your enemies! Pray for those who persecute you!"*

That's the answer to the question: We are called to do both!

Like Stephen, we must stand for truth while showing Christlike love at the same time.

It isn't easy, but it's part of being a ride or die follower of Christ.

Today's Verse:

"You have heard the law that says, 'Love your neighbor' and hate your enemy. But I say, love your enemies! Pray for those who persecute you! In that way, you will be acting as true children of your Father in heaven. For he gives his sunlight to both the evil and the good, and he sends rain on the just and the unjust alike." *(Matthew 5:43-45, NLT)*

-Jamie Holden, Founder, Mantour Ministries

Monday

Isaiah 57-58 ☐   Psalm 139 ☐

Memory Verse: *I thank my God every time I remember you. In all my prayers for all of you, I always pray with joy because of your partnership in the gospel from the first day until now,* (Philippians 1:3-5, NIV)

Tuesday

Isaiah 59-60 ☐   Proverbs 26:1-12 ☐

Memory Verse: *Being confident of this, that he who began a good work in you will carry it on to completion until the day of Christ Jesus.* (Philippians 1:6, NIV)

Wednesday

Isaiah 61-62 ☐   Psalm 139 ☐

Memory Verse: *It is right for me to feel this way about all of you, since I have you in my heart and, whether I am in chains or defending and confirming the gospel, all of you share in God's grace with me.* (Philippians 1:7, NIV)

Thursday

Isaiah 63-64 ☐   Proverbs 26:13-19 ☐

Memory Verse: *God can testify how I long for all of you with the affection of Christ Jesus.* (Philippians 1:8, NIV)

Friday

Isaiah 65-66 ☐   Psalm 140 ☐

Memory Verse: *And this is my prayer: that your love may abound more and more in knowledge and depth of insight,* (Philippians 1:9, NIV)

Saturday

1 Corinthians 1-2☐   Psalm 141☐

Memory Verse: *So that you may be able to discern what is best and may be pure and blameless for the day of Christ, filled with the fruit of righteousness that comes through Jesus Christ—to the glory and praise of God.* (Philippians 1:10-11, NIV)

THOUGHTS AND REFLECTIONS

-WEEK
FORTY-TWO-

PHINEHAS
BY JAMIE HOLDEN

Today, we're going to look at one of my heroes: Phinehas. The grandson of Aaron, his story takes place while the Israelites were wandering in the wilderness on their way to the Promised Land.

The previous chapters tell us that Israel had just been through an ordeal. The king of Moab was worried that they would attack him (even though God told them they couldn't), and he hired Balaam (the guy whose donkey talked) to curse them.

Only God wouldn't let Balaam curse them. Every time he tried, all he could do is bless Israel. (Not exactly what the king of Moab was paying him to do!)

But Balaam still had a plan. He taught the Moabites how to trap the Israelites and cause them to sin against God. The Moabite women seduced the Israelite men and caused them to participate in the sensual Moabite religious system.

The Israelite men fell into their trap. God's anger was aroused against the entire Israelite community.

God basically told them, *"Get rid of the sin or I will judge you!"*

Moses and the children of Israel obeyed God's instructions. The entire congregation was rededicated to God. They learned a hard lesson and were back on track. You would think they would never want to sin with the other nations again. Problem solved; lesson learned. I wish the story ended that way, but as we continue on, we see the opposite.

> *Then an Israelite man brought into the camp a Midianite woman right before the eyes of Moses and the whole assembly of Israel while they were weeping at the entrance to the tent of meeting. (Numbers 25:6, NIV)*

Can you believe it? Can you imagine the sheer audacity of this man? In direct defiance and rebellion to God, this man went and took his Midianite girlfriend, the daughter of the head Midianite priest, into the Tent of Meeting!

In the holy presence of God, they had sex to worship Baal!! If this wasn't offensive enough, he did it on the day that Israel was trying to get right with God and remove the sin from their lives!

If God wasn't already angry with the nation of Israel and willing to destroy them, He was now! Something had to be done—immediately!

This is where we meet Phinehas. Numbers tells us that Phinehas was so outraged that he jumped in and took action.

After seeing the horrific display of defiance against God, he was immediately filled with a righteous, holy indignation. Phinehas loved God and his nation. He couldn't stand by and let this pompous, rebellious traitor bring judgment on his people. He grabs a spear, runs up to the rebellious couple, and slams his spear directly through them both while they were having sex! WOW! I love this man.

Can you imagine how much strength it took to do this? Here's where he got it:

> *The Lord said to Moses, "Phinehas son of Eleazar, the son of Aaron, the priest, has turned my anger away*

from the Israelites. Since he was as zealous for my honor among them as I am, I did not put an end to them in my zeal. Therefore tell him I am making my covenant of peace with him. He and his descendants will have a covenant of a lasting priesthood, because he was zealous for the honor of his God and made atonement for the Israelites." (Numbers 25:10-13, NIV)

God declared that Phinehas was *"zealous with My Zeal."* He had an eager desire, an enthusiasm, to see the holiness of God defended. He loved God so much that he was jealous for God's sake. He hated that this man was, in essence, cheating on God. He felt the same pain that God was feeling, and he took action to end it.

This is part of being a ride or die man of God. While we obviously shouldn't kill people with swords (that was cultural for that time), like Phineas, we must hate evil. We cannot tolerate it. When we see sin in our lives, we must do whatever it takes to get rid of it.

Look around you. Is there something in your life that is a blatant sin against God?

Just as Phinehas used all of his strength to eliminate sin from Israel, so you need to use all of your strength to eradicate the sin in your life. We can't play around with it. We need to be passionate about living holy lives for Jesus and do whatever it takes to overcome and destroy the sin in our lives. We need to stand for God's righteousness: ride or die.

Today's Scripture:

But Phinehas stood up and intervened, and the plague was checked. This was credited to him as righteousness for endless generations to come. (Psalm 106:30-31, NIV)

-Jamie Holden, Founder, Mantour Ministries

Monday

1 Corinthians 3-4 ☐   Psalm 142 ☐

Memory Verse: *Now I want you to know, brothers and sisters, that what has happened to me has actually served to advance the gospel.* (Philippians 1:12, NIV)

Tuesday

1 Corinthians 5-6 ☐   Proverbs 26:20-28 ☐

Memory Verse: *As a result, it has become clear throughout the whole palace guard and to everyone else that I am in chains for Christ.* (Philippians 1:13, NIV)

Wednesday

1 Corinthians 7-8 ☐   Psalm 143 ☐

Memory Verse: *And because of my chains, most of the brothers and sisters have become confident in the Lord and dare all the more to proclaim the gospel without fear.* (Philippians 1:14, NIV)

Thursday

1 Corinthians 9-10 ☐   Proverbs 27:1-10 ☐

Memory Verse: *It is true that some preach Christ out of envy and rivalry, but others out of goodwill. The latter do so out of love, knowing that I am put here for the defense of the gospel.* (Philippians 1:15-16, NIV)

Friday

1 Corinthians 11-12 ☐   Psalm 144 ☐

Memory Verse: *The former preach Christ out of selfish ambition, not sincerely, supposing that they can stir up trouble for me while I am in chains.* (Philippians 1:17, NIV)

Saturday

1 Corinthians 13-14 ☐   Psalm 145 ☐

Memory Verse: *But what does it matter? The important thing is that in every way, whether from false motives or true, Christ is preached. And because of this I rejoice.* (Philippians 1:18, NIV)

-WEEK FORTY-THREE-

HEZEKIAH
BY JAMIE HOLDEN

One of my all-time favorite accounts in the Bible tells the story of King Hezekiah—one of the few truly good kings in Judea. 2 Kings 18 describes him this way:

> *"Hezekiah trusted in the Lord, the God of Israel. There was no one like him among all the kings of Judah, either before him or after him. He held fast to the Lord and did not stop following him; he kept the commands the Lord had given Moses." (2 Kings 18:5-6, NIV)*

Hezekiah was ride or die for God. God rewarded him for it. *"And the Lord was with him; he was successful in whatever he undertook. He rebelled against the king of Assyria and did not serve him." (Verse 7)*

That last line in verse 7 is really important because it introduces a new player: the king of Assyria. During Hezekiah's day, the king of Assyria was the world power conquering all the other countries. In the fourteenth year of Hezekiah's reign, the king of Assyria was coming to conquer Judea.

At first, King Hezekiah did what the Assyrian king wanted and tried to buy him off with a HUGE amount of gold and silver. But that didn't satisfy the foreign king.

Like a true bully, the king of Assyria sent his supreme commander, his chief officer, and his field commander with a large army to King Hezekiah at Jerusalem. They stood at a pivotal point in the city and called for the king. The palace administrator, secretary, and the recorder went out to them. Then they started taunting them:

"Who are you relying on to save you? None of the other nation's gods could save them. Why would you think yours can?"

"Look what happened to the other nations...it's gonna happen to you."

"Surrender to me, and I'll give you 2,000 horses...if you can find men to ride them."

Then the ultimate taunt: *"God told me to attack you. What can you do about that?"*

That's when Hezekiah's men spoke up and said, *"Could you speak Aramaic, we understand it, and you're upsetting the people?"*

But the Assyrians replied, *"We aren't just talking to you...we want to fill them with fear too."* (My paraphrase—read the whole chapter in 2 Kings 18.)

Then the Assyrians cried out in Hebrew (so everyone could hear it), *"Don't let Hezekiah deceive you...God is not going to save you. We are more powerful, and we are going to win."*

The people of Jerusalem stayed quiet, and Hezekiah tore his clothes and went into the Temple to seek God.

While Hezekiah was praying, the prophet Isaiah came in and told him to continue trusting God, and God would take care of Hezekiah and His people.

Hezekiah relied on God, and that night God slaughtered 185,000 Assyrian soldiers. The Assyrian army withdrew, and shortly after, the Assyrian king was killed by his own sons.

It's an awesome story—totally worth the time to read.

Each time I read it, I am reminded that God can be trusted. Even when the Assyrian king stood outside and hooted and howled like the big bad wolf, even when he used every fear tactic in the book to get King Hezekiah to surrender, Hezekiah choose to trust God and ride or die.

He stands as an example to us that no matter what, we can trust God. Even when the enemy seems to be screaming in your ear, *"If you trust God, if you rely on Him, He is going to let you down. God won't help you. God is against you."*

These are the times when we have to stand firm and say, "I trust God's Word. Ride or die, I believe Him, I will obey Him, and trust Him.

Today's Scripture:

Hezekiah received the letter from the messengers and read it. Then he went up to the temple of the Lord and spread it out before the Lord.

And Hezekiah prayed to the Lord: "Lord, the God of Israel, enthroned between the cherubim, you alone are God over all the kingdoms of the earth. You have made heaven and earth.

Give ear, Lord, and hear; open your eyes, Lord, and see; listen to the words Sennacherib has sent to ridicule the living God.

It is true, Lord, that the Assyrian kings have laid waste these nations and their lands. They have thrown their gods into the fire and destroyed them, for they were not gods but only wood and stone, fashioned by human hands. Now, Lord our God, deliver us from his hand, so that all the kingdoms of the earth may know that you alone, Lord, are God." (2 Kings 19:14-19, NIV)

-Jamie Holden, Founder, Mantour Ministries

Monday

1 Corinthians 15-16 ☐   Psalm 146 ☐

Memory Verse: *Yes, and I will continue to rejoice, for I know that through your prayers and God's provision of the Spirit of Jesus Christ what has happened to me will turn out for my deliverance.* (Philippians 1:18-19, NIV)

Tuesday

2 Corinthians 1-2 ☐   Proverbs 27:11-27 ☐

Memory Verse: *I eagerly expect and hope that I will in no way be ashamed, but will have sufficient courage so that now as always Christ will be exalted in my body, whether by life or by death.*
(Philippians 1:20, NIV)

Wednesday

2 Corinthians 3-4 ☐   Psalm 147 ☐

Memory Verse: *For to me, to live is Christ and to die is gain. If I am to go on living in the body, this will mean fruitful labor for me. Yet what shall I choose? I do not know!* (Philippians 1:21-22, NIV)

Thursday

2 Corinthians 5-6 ☐   Proverbs 28:1-10 ☐

Memory Verse: *I am torn between the two: I desire to depart and be with Christ, which is better by far; but it is more necessary for you that I remain in the body.* (Philippians 1:23-24 NIV)

Friday

2 Corinthians 7-8 ☐   Psalm 148 ☐

Memory Verse: *Convinced of this, I know that I will remain, and I will continue with all of you for your progress and joy in the faith,* (Philippians 1:25, NIV)

Saturday

2 Corinthians 9-10 ☐   Psalm 149 ☐

Memory Verse: *So that through my being with you again your boasting in Christ Jesus will abound on account of me.* (Philippians 1:26, NIV)

THOUGHTS AND REFLECTIONS

-WEEK FORTY-FOUR-

JAMIE HOLDEN
BY DUANE GOODLING

The task for the writers of these devotionals was to talk about people who *"demonstrated a willingness to be loyal to God, God's Word, his church, his convictions, or his family no matter what came against him."* If this doesn't describe Jamie Holden, I don't know what does. Jamie has faced many types of adversity throughout his life thus far, but continues to follow God's call on him to pursue men's ministry.

Jamie was born in 1977, and graduated from the University of Valley Forge in 1999 with a degree in pastoral ministry. Early in ministry, he spent a few years traveling with and helping his sister at women's ministry events before the Holy Spirit began speaking to him about doing events for men.

In 2013, Jamie listened to the Assemblies of God General Council meetings online when Pastor Wilfredo (Choco) De Jesús said something that impacted Jamie deeply. Pastor Choco said, *"If you don't do what the Holy Spirit is telling you to do because of fear, you shouldn't be in ministry."*

This statement spoke directly to Jamie's heart because he sensed that the Holy Spirit had been speaking to him about men's ministry. Immediately, he sent an email to Tom Rees (Assemblies of God Men's Ministry Director for Pennsylvania-Delaware Ministry Network) asking if they could get together to talk as soon as possible. Tom attended the General Council meetings in person, so they set up an appointment for the next week after he returned. Jamie went to meet

Tom with fear and trembling, but out of that meeting, he started down the path of what eventually became Mantour Ministries.

That first year, 2014, Mantour Ministries had literally no funding, and what they did have, came from a small personal savings account to pay for hotels and speakers. His sister, Adessa, told him, *"We can do four conferences—if it doesn't work, that's all the money we have, and we're not going into debt for this."* But God was faithful, and that first year they were able to hold seven events! What followed is a story that continues to be written.

Jamie eventually became an Assemblies of God US Missionary Assoc., with a commission to develop men's ministry in the local church. To go along with the Mantour Men's Conferences, Jamie writes a companion book each year to match the conference theme. He has written seven books as of 2021. The books are formatted to make them a great tool that men's ministry leaders can use in their meetings to help facilitate discussion. Jamie also raises funds to enable him to send books, free of charge, to prisons for inmates to share. Mantour Ministries is more than just a few hours on a Saturday morning.

The Mantour Men's conferences are now a standard event on Pennsylvania and Delaware men's ministry calendars. In recent years, Jamie has added conferences in Virginia and New York to the schedule. The conferences are held in strategic locations in churches around these four states, with an additional event held annually at the Adult and Teen Challenge facility in Rehrersburg, Pennsylvania. While Jamie has a heart for all men, he has put in extra work to reach men who are suffering from addiction or who are currently incarcerated.

While starting a new men's ministry can be daunting enough for anyone, Jamie was born with a hereditary, degenerative neurological disease that deforms the limbs called Charcot-Marie-Tooth disease.

Jamie lives in pain every day. While this disease specifically works in the feet and hands, it does affect other parts of his body, especially when he is tired.

While having men gather, worship, and pray all play a part in fulfilling God's call on Jamie's life, and he enjoys the conferences immensely, the events are tough on him. In fact, he often needs several days to recover physically from the toll of travel and the event itself. However, Jamie knows he is doing the will of the Lord for him, and seeing men go forward to accept Christ for the first time, makes it all worth it.

Has God spoken to you about a ministry you should start or participate? Maybe you feel it is too big or you aren't the person for the job. You may have heard the phrase *"God doesn't call the equipped; He equips the called."*

This is a true statement! If He is calling you to something, He will put the people and processes in place to help you see it through, but you must be intentional and obedient to the call. Don't take my word for it, test it out.

We all face challenges when doing ministry. Some are physical like Jamie; some are financial, and some may be unique to you, but challenges exist for us all. Are you willing to commit to God's call for you? Are you willing to trust Him as Jamie did (and still does!)? You can do it! Don't wait another day. The time is now!

Today's Scripture:

I can do all this through him who gives me strength.
(Philippians 4:13, NIV)

-Duane Goodling, Mission Director- Think Missions,
www.thinkmissions.org

Monday

2 Corinthians 11-13 ☐   Psalm 150 ☐

Memory Verse: *Whatever happens, conduct yourselves in a manner worthy of the gospel of Christ. Then, whether I come and see you or only hear about you in my absence, I will know that you stand firm in the one Spirit, striving together as one for the faith of the gospel.*
(Philippians 1:27, NIV)

Tuesday

Daniel 1-2 ☐   Psalm 1 ☐

Memory Verse: *Without being frightened in any way by those who oppose you. This is a sign to them that they will be destroyed, but that you will be saved—and that by God. (*Philippians 1:28, NIV)

Wednesday

Daniel 3-4 ☐   Proverbs 28:11-20 ☐

Memory Verse: *For it has been granted to you on behalf of Christ not only to believe in him, but also to suffer for him, since you are going through the same struggle you saw I had, and now hear that I still have. (*Philippians 1:29-30, NIV)

Thursday

Daniel 5-6 ☐   Proverbs 28:21-18 ☐

Memory Verse: *Therefore if you have any encouragement from being united with Christ, if any comfort from his love, if any common sharing in the Spirit, if any tenderness and compassion, then make my joy complete by being like-minded, having the same love, being one in spirit and of one mind.* (Philippians 2:1-2, NIV)

Friday

Revelations 1-2 ☐   Psalm 2 ☐

Memory Verse: *Do nothing out of selfish ambition or vain conceit. Rather, in humility value others above yourselves,* (Philippians 2:3, NIV)

Saturday

Revelations 3-4 ☐   Psalm 3 ☐

Memory Verse: *Not looking to your own interests but each of you to the interests of the others.* (Philippians 2:4, NIV)

THOUGHTS AND
REFLECTIONS

-WEEK FORTY-FIVE-

ABEL
BY JAMIE HOLDEN

Many of us heard the story of Cain and Abel when we were children. Sunday school stories focus on Cain—the man who brought the wrong offering, became angry with his brother who brought the right offering, lost his temper, and lured his brother into the field to kill him. For all of eternity, he is known as the world's first murderer.

Abel has a different legacy. When we read his biography in Hebrews 11, he isn't referred to as a victim of Cain's temper, but rather a righteous man who is an example of living by faith. For all of eternity, Abel stands as an example of someone whose obedience to God's ways cost him in this life but led him to rewards in the next life.

His story reminds us that evil men have hated those who obey God's ways since the beginning of time. The Bible is clear: Abel's only offense was obeying God. He followed God's commands for proper worship, while Cain chose to worship his way.

Abel did nothing wrong. He suffered for doing what was right.

Often as men of God, we, too, will suffer for doing right. While I hope none of us ever has to physically die for our commitment to obey God, many throughout history have. Whether or not we are called to pay this ultimate price, I can guarantee that there will be people who hate us for it when we walk in obedience to God's ways. It may be family, friends, co-workers, or a neighbor who hate our choice to do things God's way because it convicts them of the sin in their lives.

Choosing obedience to God may cost you friendship. Some may lose a contract or a job. Others may have to make difficult choices about whether they will continue walking in obedience to Christ or suffer significant consequences.

These are when we need to choose if we will be ride or die men of God like Abel.

Will we continue modeling righteousness or compromise for the sake of comfort?

Will we continue walking in righteousness?

Are we strong enough to be men of faith, following God even when those around us choose to disobey God and reject us for our obedience?

This is the legacy of Abel. He died for His faith. The question is: will you live for yours?

Today's Scripture:

It was by faith that Abel brought a more acceptable offering to God than Cain did. Abel's offering gave evidence that he was a righteous man, and God showed his approval of his gifts. Although Abel is long dead, he still speaks to us by his example of faith. (Hebrews 11:4, NLT)

-Jamie Holden, Founder, Mantour Ministries

Monday

Revelations 5-6 ☐   Psalm 4 ☐

Memory Verse: *In your relationships with one another, have the same mindset as Christ Jesus:* (Philippians 2:5, NIV)

Tuesday

Revelations 7-8 ☐   Psalm 5 ☐

Memory Verse: *Who, being in very nature God, did not consider equality with God something to be used to his own advantage;* (Philippians 2:6, NIV)

Wednesday

Revelations 9-10 ☐   Proverbs 29:1-12 ☐

Memory Verse: *Rather, he made himself nothing by taking the very nature of a servant, being made in human likeness.* (Philippians 2:7, NIV)

Thursday

Revelations 11-12 ☐   Proverbs 29:12-21 ☐

Memory Verse: *And being found in appearance as a man, he humbled himself by becoming obedient to death— even death on a cross!* (Philippians 2:8, NIV)

Friday

Revelations 13-14 ☐   Psalm 6 ☐

Memory Verse: *Therefore God exalted him to the highest place and gave him the name that is above every name,* (Philippians 2:9, NIV)

Saturday

Revelations 15-16☐   Psalm 7☐

Memory Verse: *That at the name of Jesus every knee should bow, in heaven and on earth and under the earth, and every tongue acknowledge that Jesus Christ is Lord, to the glory of God the Father.* (Philippians 2:10-11, NIV)

THOUGHTS AND REFLECTIONS

-ᗯᗴᗴK ᖴOᖇTY-ᔕᓰ᙭-

RIDE OR DIE TOGETHER
BY GREG NASS

Mountain biking at a new location is always exciting because I ride new trails and see new sights. Then when I get the opportunity to go at it alone, that adventure level quickly jumps from awesome to epic as I anticipate and prepare for the unexpected.

Having the proper tools on hand in case something breaks could be critical to survival, as some trails can take you miles and miles away from civilization. I recently went to a new trail system in the mountains of Pennsylvania. After about 12 miles into the ride, I developed a creak coming from my drivetrain - the drivetrain is all the parts that make you go, including the pedals, cranks, sprockets, and chain. Climbing a big hill, my chain broke, throwing me forward and down into the bike, which is startling and painful. Without the chain, my bike won't move. Thankfully, I prepared and brought a chain tool that helped me repair a broken link. I was able to fix my chain and get going again.

That broken chain made me think about 1 Corinthians 12:12-19. It reminded me that we are all part of one body. My bike is useless without a chain. It's also useless without a tire or a pedal because it all works together to move the bike forward. If one is down, they're all down. On the flip side of that coin, if all parts work together in harmony, the bike functions as it should and allows for adrenaline-pumping travel.

Just like the pieces on my bike, we are all part of the body of our Lord and Savior, Jesus Christ. We all have a unique purpose, one that has been gifted to us by God. When coupled with others' unique purpose, it now becomes even more powerful, and it's all for the glory of Jesus Christ.

That's why we need to stay connected to the other parts of the body of Christ. We can't function alone--we need to ride together!

Today's Scripture:

Just as a body, though one, has many parts, but all its many parts form one body, so it is with Christ. For we were all baptized by one Spirit so as to form one body—whether Jews or Gentiles, slave or free—and we were all given the one Spirit to drink. Even so the body is not made up of one part but of many.

Now if the foot should say, "Because I am not a hand, I do not belong to the body," it would not for that reason stop being part of the body. And if the ear should say, "Because I am not an eye, I do not belong to the body," it would not for that reason stop being part of the body.

If the whole body were an eye, where would the sense of hearing be? If the whole body were an ear, where would the sense of smell be?

But in fact God has placed the parts in the body, every one of them, just as he wanted them to be. If they were all one part, where would the body be? (1 Corinthians 12:12-19, NIV)

Greg Nass, Founder, AdventureMen Ministries
https://www.adventuremen.org

Monday

Revelations 17-18☐   Psalm 8 ☐

Memory Verse: *Therefore, my dear friends, as you have always obeyed—not only in my presence, but now much more in my absence—continue to work out your salvation with fear and trembling,*(Philippians 2:12, NIV)

Tuesday

Revelations 19-20☐   Proverbs 29:22-27 ☐

Memory Verse: *For it is God who works in you to will and to act in order to fulfill his good purpose.* (Philippians 2:13, NIV)

Wednesday

Revelations 21-22☐   Psalm 9 ☐

Memory Verse: *Do everything without grumbling or arguing, so that you may become blameless and pure, "children of God without fault in a warped and crooked generation."* (Philippians 2:14-15, NIV)

Thursday

Hosea 1-2 ☐   Proverbs 30:1-4 ☐

Memory Verse: *Then you will shine among them like stars in the sky as you hold firmly to the word of life. And then I will be able to boast on the day of Christ that I did not run or labor in vain.*(Philippians 2:15-16, NIV)

Friday

Hosea 3-4 ☐   Psalm 10 ☐

Memory Verse: *But even if I am being poured out like a drink offering on the sacrifice and service coming from your faith, I am glad and rejoice with all of you.* (Philippians 2:17, NIV)

Saturday

Hosea 5-6 ☐   Psalm 11 ☐

Memory Verse: *So you too should be glad and rejoice with me.* (Philippians 2:18, NIV)

-WEEK FORTY-SEVEN-

PETER AND JESUS: READINESS TO DIE
BY SCOTT A. GRAY

It's a serious action when you make a vow to God. It's a solemn promise, not a nonchalant attitude. Have you ever promised someone that you would do a specific thing, but you ended up breaking your promise? Failure certainly brings a feeling of tremendous disappointment or despair.

People have often said, *"Don't make a promise that you can't keep."* At first glance, this saying appears to mean you shouldn't make promises altogether. However, it means rather you should be circumspect in making promises; that is, you should think carefully before saying anything. The Bible says, **"When you make a vow to God, do not delay to fulfill it. He has no pleasure in fools; fulfill your vow" (Ecclesiastes 5:4, NIV).**

There was a man in the Bible that made a bold, blatant promise to Jesus. His name was Peter. His promise was the very essence of what a ride or die mentality looks like.

But Peter declared, **"Even if I have to die with you, I will never disown you." And all the other disciples said the same. (Matthew 26:35, NIV).**

Not only was Peter willing to die for Jesus, but all the disciples said they were willing to die, too. If Peter promised, the other disciples couldn't promise anything less. Once the heart is fully committed, the action will soon follow. Many people have laid down their lives for what they believe in, either religiously or sacrificially, for someone else to live. Peter was willing to lay down his life for his Master because of what he saw, touched, and heard. To Peter, Jesus was *"the Christ, the Messiah, the Son of the living God." (Matthew 16:16, MSG)*

His promise wasn't to die for a belief, concept, opinion, or philosophy, but rather to die for a person whom he loved immensely. Jesus himself said, *"Greater love has no one than this: to lay down one's life for one's friends." (John 15:13, NIV)*

Love is a powerful action on behalf of another and is expressed in a myriad of ways. It compels people to take extraordinary measures. So, the basis of a ride or die mentality is the love of God flowing through us.

What is the love of God? God takes us to the cross of Christ and declares, *"this is love."* It's about unswerving sacrifice, surrender, obedience, and loyalty.

We don't know whether Peter answered hastily or gave it some thought, but his statement demonstrated his readiness to die with Jesus. Notice that Peter didn't say, *"Even if I have to die for you..."* He said with Jesus. (Matthew 26:35; Mark 14:31; Luke 22:33) In Luke's gospel, Peter said to Jesus that he would be *"ready to go with you both to prison and to death."*

But in John 13:37, Peter said he would die for Jesus. *"Peter said to him, 'Lord, why can't I not follow you now? I will lay down my life for You'". (NIV)*

A few hours later, we find the disciples not sacrificing their lives for Jesus but running to save their lives! Peter vowed to be faithful. They say that *"talk is cheap."* It's easy for anyone to proclaim their devotion to Christ by their words, but when your life is under pressure, or you are in a peculiar situation, the test is given by God to see if our words are true and meaningful. God wants you to find out how strong your faith really is.

According to church tradition, Peter died as a martyr for Jesus in Rome under Emperor Nero. He was crucified upside down because he felt unworthy to die in the same manner as Jesus. Peter really was Jesus' ride or die friend because Peter had learned the truth of Jesus' words in Matthew 10:39, ***"Whoever finds their life will lose it, and whoever loses their life for my sake will find it"*** (NIV).

Today's Scripture:

Greater love has no one than this: to lay down one's life for one's friends. (John 15:13, NIV)

-Scott A. Gray, Associate Pastor, Lighthouse Church

Monday

Hosea 7-8 ☐   Psalm 12 ☐

Memory Verse: *I hope in the Lord Jesus to send Timothy to you soon, that I also may be cheered when I receive news about you. I have no one else like him, who will show genuine concern for your welfare.* (Philippians 2:19-20, NIV)

Tuesday

Hosea 9-10 ☐   Proverbs 30:5-6 ☐

Memory Verse: *For everyone looks out for their own interests, not those of Jesus Christ. But you know that Timothy has proved himself, because as a son with his father he has served with me in the work of the gospel. I hope, therefore, to send him as soon as I see how things go with me. And I am confident in the Lord that I myself will come soon.* (Philippians 2:21-24, NIV)

Wednesday

Hosea 11-12 ☐ Psalm 13 ☐

Memory Verse: *But I think it is necessary to send back to you Epaphroditus, my brother, co-worker and fellow soldier, who is also your messenger, whom you sent to take care of my needs. For he longs for all of you and is distressed because you heard he was ill.* (Philippians 2:25-26, NIV)

Thursday

Habakkuk ☐ Proverbs 30:7-10 ☐

Memory Verse: *Indeed he was ill, and almost died. But God had mercy on him, and not on him only but also on me, to spare me sorrow upon sorrow.* (Philippians 2:27, NIV)

Friday

Joel 1-2 ☐ Psalm 14 ☐

Memory Verse: *Therefore I am all the more eager to send him, so that when you see him again you may be glad and I may have less anxiety.* (Philippians 2:28, NIV)

Saturday

Joel 3 ☐ Obadiah ☐ Psalm 15 ☐

Memory Verse: *So then, welcome him in the Lord with great joy, and honor people like him, because he almost died for the work of Christ. He risked his life to make up for the help you yourselves could not give me.* (Philippians 2:29-30, NIV)

-WEEK FORTY-EIGHT-

RIDE OR DIE FOR GOD'S WORD
BY WAYNE SCHAFFER

Redefine, reprogram, reeducate, redistribute— the *"RE's"* are at it again. This isn't the first, and it won't be the last time in human history that an attempt has been made to alter and cancel God's truth and God's people. Every time an attempt has been made, God's Word has prevailed. God's people persevered through it, and God's purposes were fulfilled.

> *"If you continue in your faith, established and firm, and do not move from the hope held out in the gospel. This is the gospel that you heard and that has been proclaimed to every creature under heaven, and of which I, Paul, have become a servant."*
> *(Colossians 1:23, NIV)*

Pharaoh wanted to kill the Hebrew children. (Exodus 1:15-22)

Herod wanted to kill the Hebrew boys. (Matt. 2:16-18)

Today we want to kill the unborn (abortion) and even the born with (gender identity). The world has always tried to silence those who proclaim God's Word.

Jezebel set out to kill God's prophets. (1 Kings 18:4)

The teachers of the law sought to kill Jesus. (Matt. 23:29-36)

All of the Apostles died a martyr's death.

Today, anyone who dares speak the truth is under attack, being canceled, put in Facebook jail, deleted from social media, mocked, and ridiculed. And yet, we are called upon as Christians not to respond with evil.

> *Do not repay anyone evil for evil. Be careful to do what is right in the eyes of everyone. If it is possible, as far as it depends on you, live at peace with everyone.*
>
> *Do not take revenge, my dear friends, but leave room for God's wrath, for it is written: "It is mine to avenge; I will repay," says the Lord.*
>
> *On the contrary: "If your enemy is hungry, feed him; if he is thirsty, give him something to drink. In doing this, you will heap burning coals on his head." Do not be overcome by evil, but overcome evil with good. (Romans 12:17-21, NIV)*

The world has tried to eliminate the Bible's existence.

King Jehoiakim hated the Word of God. He ordered it to be cut, burned and ordered the arrest of Jeremiah. (Jeremiah 36)

Today, we find ourselves faced with those who are trying to redefine truth and silence the Gospel. They want to reduce the Bible to nothing more than a fictitious storybook. Freedom to preach God's Word is under attack worldwide, and it's starting to happen in the US and Canada.

There are calls to silence the Bible's moral clarity on many topics (Marriage, LGBTQ, abortion, socialism, salvation). If you speak God's truth, it is almost certain that it will be lampooned as *"hate speech."*

So what will you do? Will you conform to the world, or will you contend for the faith?

"I...urge you to contend for the faith that was once for all entrusted to God's holy people." (Jude 3, NIV)

Revelation 12:17 tells us, **"Those who keep God's commands and hold fast their testimony about Jesus"** are at war with Satan. He will use every force of this present age to battle against God's Word and God's people. While our current culture is attempting to silence the truth and brand its *"lies"* as the *"new truth,"* as Christians, we must hold fast to The Truth!

Though it may be hard, I find that 1 Peter 2:15 gives us a way to defeat those who are trying to silence us, **"by doing good you put to silence the ignorance of foolish men." (1 Pet. 2:15, NIV)**

Truly the only *"RE"* that should be happening is the RENEWING of our mind, **"Do not conform to the pattern of this world, but be transformed by the renewing of your mind. Then you will be able to test and approve what God's will is—his good, pleasing and perfect will." (Romans 12:2)**

Today's Scripture:

If you continue in your faith, established and firm, and do not move from the hope held out in the gospel. This is the gospel that you heard and that has been proclaimed to every creature under heaven, and of which I, Paul, have become a servant. (Colossians 1:23, NIV)

-Wayne Schaffer, Pastor New Life Worship Center in Altoona, PA, Presbyter, South Central West Section PennDel Assembly of God

Monday

1 Chronicles 10-11 ☐   Psalm 16 ☐

Memory Verse: *Further, my brothers and sisters, rejoice in the Lord! It is no trouble for me to write the same things to you again, and it is a safeguard for you.* (Philippians 3:1, NIV)

Tuesday

1 Chronicles 12-13 ☐   Proverbs 30:11-14 ☐

Memory Verse: *Watch out for those dogs, those evildoers, those mutilators of the flesh.* (Philippians 3:2, NIV)

Wednesday

1 Chronicles 14-15 ☐   Psalm 17 ☐

Memory Verse: *For it is we who are the circumcision, we who serve God by his Spirit, who boast in Christ Jesus, and who put no confidence in the flesh* (Philippians 3:3, NIV)

Thursday

1 Chronicles 16-17 ☐   Proverbs 30:15-17 ☐

Memory Verse: *Though I myself have reasons for such confidence. If someone else thinks they have reasons to put confidence in the flesh, I have more: circumcised on the eighth day, of the people of Israel, of the tribe of Benjamin, a Hebrew of Hebrews; in regard to the law, a Pharisee; as for zeal, persecuting the church; as for righteousness based on the law, faultless.* (Philippians 3:4-6, NIV)

Friday

1 Chronicles 18-19 ☐   Psalm 18 ☐

Memory Verse: *But whatever were gains to me I now consider loss for the sake of Christ.* (Philippians 3:7, NIV)

Saturday

1 Chronicles 20-21 ☐   Psalm 19 ☐

Memory Verse: *What is more, I consider everything a loss because of the surpassing worth of knowing Christ Jesus my Lord, for whose sake I have lost all things. I consider them garbage, that I may gain Christ.* (Philippians 3:8, NIV)

WEEK FORTY-NINE

JESUS
BY JAMIE HOLDEN

It is impossible to write a book about ride or die men of God without including the ultimate example, Jesus.

Philippians 2 tells us that to fulfill His purpose, Jesus had first to give up a lot.

> *Who, being in very nature God, did not consider equality with God something to be used to his own advantage; rather, he made himself nothing by taking the very nature of a servant, being made in human likeness.*
>
> *And being found in appearance as a man, he humbled himself by becoming obedient to death- (Philippians 2:6-8, NIV)*

This time of year, we focus on the birth of Christ. Yet, before Jesus was born, He made a ride or die choice to give up all of Heaven and come to earth.

He left the perfection, the grandeur, the beauty of Heaven to come and be born in a stable to poor Jewish parents.

Even though He was God, He took on a human body. Even though He couldn't get sick, He could feel pain, exhaustion, heartache, and a full range of emotions.

He grew up a Jewish man in a world dominated by the Roman

Empire.

Even though He created everything and was literally the king of the world, He took on the form of a servant. As a man, He worked hard, He paid bills, and until He was thirty years old, He had the responsibility to provide for His Mom and siblings.

During His ministry, He suffered hatred and persecution from the religious leaders and chose to reach out and touch the common person.

He suffered betrayal by one of His disciples and was let down by all of His closest friends.

Yet, He chose to ride and die so that God's purpose could be fulfilled.

Jesus was born for one purpose and one purpose only. He knew what His purpose was, and He chose to ride or die to fulfill His purpose.

Jesus was born to be the needed sacrifice for man's sins. He was born to live and die for every one of us. The only way we could be reunited with God was for Jesus to take on humanity to die for our sins. He was the only one who could do it. He faced mocking, ridicule, and even persecution as He walked the earth, but He chose to ride or die with his Father's purpose.

Even in the garden of Gethsemane, He said to his Father, *"Not My will, but Your will be done."* He was basically saying, *"Father, is there any chance I don't have to do this…but if I must, I will ride or die with You and the purpose You have given to Me."*

Jesus went to the cross to fulfill His purpose. Even on the cross, beaten and abused, He faced the temptation to give up on His purpose. *"Come down from the cross if You're all You claim to be,"* they mocked and jeered.

Jesus could have come right off of that cross. He had the power to send an army of angels to silence His enemies. But with a ride or die sense of purpose, He ignored their taunts. His work was too great, and He couldn't come down!

Jesus is the ultimate ride or die man of God.

Today, a risen Jesus challenges all of us to follow His example and give everything to God just as He gave everything to us.

Following His example, today, you must decide that your work, your purpose, the one thing God created you to do, is too vital for you to surrender. You cannot come down!

You must choose, like Jesus, to commit yourself to discover what your true purpose is in life. Then you must choose to give it all you got.

No matter what obstacles you face or what comes against you, you must ride or die with purpose.

Like Jesus, each of us must submit our will to God and say, *"Not my will, but Your will, be done in my life. Whatever You ask, I'll ride or die with You to the end."*

Today's Scripture:

Have the same mindset as Christ Jesus: Who, being in very nature God, did not consider equality with God something to be used to his own advantage; rather, he made himself nothing by taking the very nature of a servant, being made in human likeness. And being found in appearance as a man, he humbled himself by becoming obedient to death—even death on a cross!

Therefore God exalted him to the highest place and gave him the name that is above every name, that at the name of Jesus every knee should bow, in heaven and on earth and under the earth, and every tongue acknowledge that Jesus Christ is Lord, to the glory of God the Father. (Philippians 2:5-11, NIV)

-Jamie Holden, Founder, Mantour Ministries

Monday

1 Chronicles 22 ☐   1 Chronicles 28 ☐   Psalm 20 ☐

Memory Verse: *And be found in him, not having a righteousness of my own that comes from the law, but that which is through faith in Christ—the righteousness that comes from God on the basis of faith.* (Philippians 3:9, NIV)

Tuesday

1 Chronicles 29 ☐   2 Chronicles 1 ☐   Proverbs 30:18-19 ☐

Memory Verse: *I want to know Christ—yes, to know the power of his resurrection and participation in his sufferings, becoming like him in his death, and so, somehow, attaining to the resurrection from the dead.* (Philippians 3:10-11, NIV)

Wednesday

2 Chronicles 2-3 ☐   Psalm 21 ☐

Memory Verse: *Not that I have already obtained all this, or have already arrived at my goal, but I press on to take hold of that for which Christ Jesus took hold of me.* (Philippians 3:12, NIV)

Thursday

2 Chronicles 5-6 ☐   Proverbs 30:20-23 ☐

Memory Verse: *Brothers and sisters, I do not consider myself yet to have taken hold of it. But one thing I do: Forgetting what is behind and straining toward what is ahead, I press on toward the goal to win the prize for which God has called me heavenward in Christ Jesus.* (Philippians 3:13-14, NIV)

Friday

2 Chronicles 7-9 ☐   Psalm 22 ☐

Memory Verse: *All of us, then, who are mature should take such a view of things. And if on some point you think differently, that too God will make clear to you.* (Philippians 3:15, NIV)

Saturday

2 Chronicles 24-26 ☐   Psalm 23 ☐

Memory Verse: *Only let us live up to what we have already attained.* (Philippians 3:16, NIV)

THOUGHTS AND

REFLECTIONS

-WEEK FIFTY-

WISE MEN
BY JAMIE HOLDEN

I can almost see it now—a group of astrologers sitting around talking about the star that appeared over Bethlehem.

"That star is amazing."

"I wonder what it means."

"Wouldn't it be great to go and see?"

Before long, they have their hands in the air, giving high-fives as they said, *"Road Trip!!!"*

Okay, maybe my description of the wise men is a little more American cowboy than ancient Eastern, but you have to admit, this was the ultimate road trip!   Researchers aren't exactly sure, but the estimates range from 40 days to 2 years of travel!   (That's a looong trip.)

Shortly after they arrived in Jerusalem, Matthew tells us that King Herod wanted to speak to them secretly. He'd heard about their trip and was very disturbed, but he didn't want them to know that. Instead, he pretended like he, too, wanted to meet the new king so he could worship Him. He told them to let them know as soon as they found the baby.

But there was just something about King Herod that the wise men didn't trust. Again, I can hear their conversation:

"Dude," (because all wise men call each other 'dude') *"Was there something weird about that guy?"*

"Yeah, he seemed a little crazy to me. Nut-job!"

"There's just something about him I don't trust."

Moving on from King Herod, the wise men continued following the star until they found the home of Mary, Joseph, and the One they were searching for: Jesus.

Matthew tells us, "**On coming to the house, they saw the child with his mother Mary, and they bowed down and worshiped him. Then they opened their treasures and presented him with gifts of gold, frankincense, and myrrh.**

And having been warned in a dream not to go back to Herod, they returned to their country by another route." **(Matthew 2:11-12, NIV)**

So what does this story have to do with being a ride or die man of God?

We often read these verses as part of the Christmas story without really thinking about the danger the wise men put themselves in by choosing to disobey Herod. Their role in the Christmas pageant concludes after they arrive in their elaborate costumes and give their gold, frankincense, and myrrh. Then their curtain falls, and we all eat Christmas cookies.

However, their story continued in real life as they chose to obey God's warning that Herod wanted to kill Jesus. (Matthew 2:13) When they decided to go in another direction, we can assume that King Herod, who was known to execute people (including one of his wives), was furious with them! By going another direction, they put their own lives at risk.

Yet, they still obeyed God.

There are several lessons we can learn from the story of the wise men:

First, God's plans aren't always the same as our plans. The wise men were on a journey to find a new king. Instead, they met crazy king Herod and a baby living in a house with his parents. Not exactly what they were expecting.

Second, God's plans for our lives often carry a more significant purpose than we plan.

We don't know what the wise men intended when they brought their gifts to Jesus. However, I doubt they ever imagined that their gifts would provide a poor Jewish couple with the means to escape an evil king and sustain themselves for two years in Egypt. Yet, that was God's plan. He took their gift and used it to preserve the Messiah who would die for the sins of the world. I'm sure that's more than they EVER imagined.

Finally, following God isn't always the easy road we expect.

When the wise men left their home, I'm sure they thought they'd anticipated everything they needed for their journey. Water, food, money, supplies...they thought they'd planned for it all. Still, I'm sure they never planned for a crazy king who wanted to annihilate babies. I'm sure they didn't plan for God to warn them in a dream to go a different route and disobey the king. All of these were God-ordained detours.

What made the wise men ride or die was that they followed God's plan and obeyed Him.

Today, they inspire us to be men who are willing to obey God even when He changes our plans. When He asks us to travel a more challenging road, even a road that seems more dangerous, will we obey, believing that He knows best?

Will we follow not just a star but the One Who created the stars, wherever, whenever He leads—ride or die?

Are you ready for the ultimate adventure…following God no matter what?

Today's Verse:

After Jesus was born in Bethlehem in Judea, during the time of King Herod, Magi from the east came to Jerusalem and asked, "Where is the one who has been born king of the Jews? We saw his star when it rose and have come to worship him."

When King Herod heard this he was disturbed, and all Jerusalem with him. When he had called together all the people's chief priests and teachers of the law, he asked them where the Messiah was to be born….

…After they had heard the king, they went on their way, and the star they had seen when it rose went ahead of them until it stopped over the place where the child was. When they saw the star, they were overjoyed.

On coming to the house, they saw the child with his mother Mary, and they bowed down and worshiped him. Then they opened their treasures and presented him with gifts of gold, frankincense and myrrh. And having been warned in a dream not to go back to Herod, they returned to their country by another route. (Matthew 2:1-4 and 9-12, NIV)

-Jamie Holden, Founder, Mantour Ministries

Monday

2 Chronicles 27-28 ☐   Psalm 24 ☐

Memory Verse: *Join together in following my example, brothers and sisters, and just as you have us as a model, keep your eyes on those who live as we do.* (Philippians 3:17, NIV)

Tuesday

2 Chronicles 30-32 ☐   Proverbs 30:24-28 ☐

Memory Verse: *For, as I have often told you before and now tell you again even with tears, many live as enemies of the cross of Christ.* (Philippians 3:18, NIV)

Wednesday

2 Chronicles 33-34 ☐   Psalm 25 ☐

Memory Verse: *Their destiny is destruction, their god is their stomach, and their glory is in their shame. Their mind is set on earthly things.* (Philippians 3:19, NIV)

Thursday

2 Chronicles 35-36 ☐   Proverbs 30:29-31 ☐

Memory Verse: *But our citizenship is in heaven. And we eagerly await a Savior from there, the Lord Jesus Christ, who, by the power that enables him to bring everything under his control, will transform our lowly bodies so that they will be like his glorious body.* (Philippians 3:20-21, NIV)

Friday

Matthew 1-2 ☐   Psalm 26 ☐

Memory Verse: *Therefore, my brothers and sisters, you whom I love and long for, my joy and crown, stand firm in the Lord in this way, dear friends!* (Philippians 4:1, NIV)

Saturday

Matthew 3-4 ☐   Psalm 27 ☐

Memory Verse: *I plead with Euodia and I plead with Syntyche to be of the same mind in the Lord. Yes, and I ask you, my true companion, help these women since they have contended at my side in the cause of the gospel, along with Clement and the rest of my co-workers, whose names are in the book of life.* (Philippians 4:2-3, NIV)

THOUGHTS AND

REFLECTIONS

WEEK FIFTY-ONE-

JOSEPH
BY JAMIE HOLDEN

I love Christmas! Everyone who sees me in December knows it!

How? Well, first, I've made it a tradition to wear Christmas t-shirts every day after November. (Unless I'm speaking at a church —then I wear my Christmas sweater!) Our house is decorated with Christmas lights. Drive past my car, and you'll hear Christmas music blasting. Of course, my sister has Hallmark movies almost on a loop at our house. (Maybe I watch a few...and by a few, I mean most of them...and no, you cannot have my mancard!)

I love celebrating this season. Yet, I know that these things are only the bells and whistles of the real reason for the season...God sent His Son to earth as a man to save all of mankind from their sins.

This week's ride or die man of God was a central figure in the miracle...Joseph. Joseph wasn't just riding or dying for God; he also rode or died for his family.

From the moment the angel appeared to Joseph and told him that Mary was pregnant through the Holy Spirit and her baby would be the Messiah, Joseph immediately took the mantle of responsibility for Mary and Jesus.

First, he married her. This was HUGE in their society. An unwed mother in their time should have been stoned to death. When Joseph married her, he saved her life.

Joseph also protected God's plan and miracle by exhibiting self-control and waiting until after Jesus was born to consummate their marriage. Even though physical intimacy was off the table for a time, Joseph still loved Mary, provided for her, and protected her in every way a man should.

He took her with him to Bethlehem for the census. After Jesus was born, he provided Mary and Jesus with a home, provided for them, and gave them stability for around three years.

Then came the strange knock at the door. It was wise men from the East who come to worship Jesus. Joseph had to wonder what was happening when they brought their expensive gifts.

Of course, he didn't have to wonder long. After they were gone, an angel came and told Joseph, ***"Get up," he said, "take the child and his mother and escape to Egypt. Stay there until I tell you, for Herod is going to search for the child to kill him." (Matthew 2:13, NIV)***

Again, Joseph obeyed God and left his home, his business, and the life they created and moved to the foreign country of Egypt to protect his family. They lived there for about three years before the king died, and it was safe to move back to Israel. This time they moved to Nazareth...another new town, another new business. Yet, Joseph did whatever was necessary to take care of his family.

That's just the kind of man Joseph was. As we continue to read Scripture, we see that Joseph worked hard to take care of his family until he died. He loved Mary, and they had other children. He raised Jesus as his own son. He taught Jesus to be a carpenter and left the family business to Him. He even took responsibility to train his family in spiritual matters by taking them to Jerusalem every year for the Passover Festival. (Luke 2:41)

Joseph sets an example that all men can follow to be ride or die for God and our families. He reminds us that this is every man's calling: to love, protect, and provide for the people God puts in our lives.

We follow his example by taking our wedding vows seriously and choosing to love, honor, protect, and respect our wives. When you follow the command in Ephesians 5 to love your wives as Christ loved the church. When you obey Ephesians 6:4 and bring up your children to serve God.

When you lead your family in following Christ and make God's ways the center of your family, as it says in Deuteronomy 6.

For those who are not married, you follow Joseph's example when you honor your parents and provide every woman and child in your life with a safe and protected environment. Women should never feel like they are in danger or threatened by a man of God. They should trust us as they would a faithful brother or father. Married or single, you should provide a godly example for children to follow.

Joseph is such a great example of how to be ride or die men who are faithful to God and our families.

It's the responsibility of every man of God.

Today's Scripture:

This is how the birth of Jesus the Messiah came about: His mother Mary was pledged to be married to Joseph, but before they came together, she was found to be pregnant through the Holy Spirit. Because Joseph her husband was faithful to the law, and yet did not want to expose her to public disgrace, he had in mind to divorce her quietly.

But after he had considered this, an angel of the Lord appeared to him in a dream and said, "Joseph son of David, do not be afraid to take Mary home as your wife, because what is conceived in her is from the Holy Spirit. She will give birth to a son, and you are to give him the name Jesus, because he will save his people from their sins."

...When Joseph woke up, he did what the angel of the Lord had commanded him and took Mary home as his wife. But he did not consummate their marriage until she gave birth to a son. And he gave him the name Jesus. (Matthew 1:18-21 and 24-25, NIV)

-Jamie Holden, Founder, Mantour Ministries

Monday

Matthew 5-6 ☐   Psalm 28 ☐

Memory Verse: *Rejoice in the Lord always. I will say it again: Rejoice!* (Philippians 4:4, NIV)

Tuesday

Matthew 7-8 ☐   Proverbs 30:32-33 ☐

Memory Verse: *Let your gentleness be evident to all. The Lord is near.* (Philippians 4:5, NIV)

Wednesday

Matthew 8-9 ☐   Psalm 29:1-5 ☐

Memory Verse: *Do not be anxious about anything, but in every situation, by prayer and petition, with thanksgiving, present your requests to God.* (Philippians 4:6, NIV)

Thursday

Matthew 10-11 ☐   Psalm 29:6-11 ☐

Memory Verse: *And the peace of God, which transcends all understanding, will guard your hearts and your minds in Christ Jesus.* (Philippians 4:7, NIV)

Friday

Matthew 12-13 ☐   Proverbs 31:1-9 ☐

Memory Verse: *Finally, brothers and sisters, whatever is true, whatever is noble, whatever is right, whatever is pure, whatever is lovely, whatever is admirable—if anything is excellent or praiseworthy—think about such things.* (Philippians 4:8, NIV)

Saturday

Matthew 14-15 ☐   Psalm 30 ☐

Memory Verse: *Whatever you have learned or received or heard from me, or seen in me—put it into practice. And the God of peace will be with you.* (Philippians 4:9, NIV)

THOUGHTS AND
REFLECTIONS

-WEEK FIFTY-TWO-

CONCLUSION: WILL YOU RIDE OR DIE?

I could go on and on, but I've run out of time. There are so many more—Gideon, Barak, Samson, Jephthah, David, Samuel, the prophets. ...Through acts of faith, they toppled kingdoms, made justice work, took the promises for themselves. They were protected from lions, fires, and sword thrusts, turned disadvantage to advantage, won battles, routed alien armies. Women received their loved ones back from the dead. There were those who, under torture, refused to give in and go free, preferring something better: resurrection. Others braved abuse and whips, and, yes, chains and dungeons. We have stories of those who were stoned, sawed in two, murdered in cold blood; stories of vagrants wandering the earth in animal skins, homeless, friendless, powerless—the world didn't deserve them!—making their way as best they could on the cruel edges of the world. -Hebrews 11:32-38 (The Message)

We have reached the end of our time together in this Bible Plan. For fifty-two weeks, we have looked at men who made similar choices to ride or die with reckless abandon for God throughout history. Each one chose to ride and die with God when faced with life's tough decisions and situations.

They were all ordinary men, just like you and me. But their decision to ride for God raised them from the status of ordinary guys to extraordinary living legends in God's Kingdom. Just like us, they faced trials, struggles, temptations, and tendencies that had the potential to destroy their walk with God. But each of them stood through the tests and became men we can pattern our spiritual journeys after.

These are just a few stories. Hebrews 11, which started this devotional, says what could easily be said about this book. I don't have time to tell you about every man and woman of God in the Bible and throughout history who has made that decision that, no matter what, I will ride or die with God! History is full of them. You know what, you could also join their ranks as you decide to ride or die with God!

I hope this book has inspired you to make the choices they made, that no matter what they encountered, what trials they faced, or whatever God required of them, they would ride or die with Him!

As you daily choose to live with a ride-or-die attitude, you could be the legend future generations admire.

This is what it is all about. Just as they rode and died with God, inspiring us to follow their example, and we need to do the same for the next generation.

Just as we look to those who have gone before us, they need to be able to look to us for inspiration. The next generation needs us to demonstrate how to be a ride or die Christian. We can become spiritual legends for the next generation, and God's Kingdom will grow stronger.

We have a world of young men and women growing up without a strong, Christ-like male role model. We can be a living example of how to walk with God, surrender completely to Him, and trust Him no matter what. They can learn from us how to hear God's voice and respond to His call. They can see us hear God's challenge and watch us fist-pump God and say, *"No matter what, I will ride and die with you!"* and be inspired to do the same.

So I end this year's plan with the same questions I asked earlier. Have you been challenged this year to choose to have a ride-or-die attitude with God no matter what you are going through? Will you decide that there is nothing God could ask of you that you would not be willing to do? If it means you will go to the ends of the earth for God and taking risks for Him, will you stand by Him and for Him no matter the cost? Will you ride with Him even if it ends up killing you?

I want to end this plan with the same challenge we started out asking. Will you make a statement of extreme loyalty and devotion to God, no matter what He does, where He leads, or what He asks of you?

Will you ride or die with God? I know my decision, what is yours?

Today's Scripture:

All these people earned a good reputation because of their faith, yet none of them received all that God had promised. For God had something better in mind for us, so that they would not reach perfection without us. (Hebrews 11:39-40, NLT)

-Jamie Holden, Founder, Mantour Ministries

Monday

Matthew 17-18 ☐   Psalm 31 ☐

Memory Verse: *I rejoiced greatly in the Lord that at last you renewed your concern for me. Indeed, you were concerned, but you had no opportunity to show it. I am not saying this because I am in need, for I have learned to be content whatever the circumstances.*
(Philippians 4:10-11, NIV)

Tuesday

Matthew 19-20 ☐   Psalm 32 ☐

Memory Verse: *I know what it is to be in need, and I know what it is to have plenty. I have learned the secret of being content in any and every situation, whether well fed or hungry, whether living in plenty or in want. I can do all this through him who gives me strength.*
(Philippians 4:12-13, NIV)

Wednesday

Matthew 21-22 ☐   Proverbs 31:10-31 ☐

Memory Verse: *Yet it was good of you to share in my troubles.*
(Philippians 4:14, NIV)

Thursday

Matthew 23-24 ☐   Psalm 33 ☐

Memory Verse: *Moreover, as you Philippians know, in the early days of your acquaintance with the gospel, when I set out from Macedonia, not one church shared with me in the matter of giving and receiving, except you only; for even when I was in Thessalonica, you sent me aid more than once when I was in need.* (Philippians 4:15-16, NIV)

Friday

Matthew 25-26 ☐   Psalm 34 ☐

Memory Verse: *Not that I desire your gifts; what I desire is that more be credited to your account. I have received full payment and have more than enough. I am amply supplied, now that I have received from Epaphroditus the gifts you sent. They are a fragrant offering, an acceptable sacrifice, pleasing to God.* (Philippians 4:17-18, NIV)

Saturday

Matthew 27-28 ☐   Psalm 35 ☐

Memory Verse: *And my God will meet all your needs according to the riches of his glory in Christ Jesus. To our God and Father be glory for ever and ever. Amen.* (Philippians 4:19-20, NIV)

THOUGHTS AND

REFLECTIONS

BIBLIOGRAPHY

Introduction

1. "ride or die." Dictionary.com. dictionary.com, LLC, 2011.

https://www.dictionary.com/e/slang/ride-or-die/. Accessed: 30 August 2021.

2."ride or die." urbandictionary.com. Urban Dictionary, 1999-2021. https://www.urbandictionary.comdefine.phpterm=ride%20or%20die, Accessed: 30 August 2021.

Chapter 12

1. "ride or die." urbandictionary.com. Urban Dictionary, 1999-2021. https://www.urbandictionary.comdefine.phpterm =ride%20or%20die, Accessed: 30 August 2021.

Chapter 26

1.Washington, Booker T. "Up From Slavery". New York: Doubleday, 2000.

Chapter 38

1."Rival" Merriam-Webster.com. Merriam Webster,

https://www.merriam-webster.com/dictionary/rival, Accessed 1 September 2021.

Chapter 39

1.Van Dyke, Michael. "Radical Integrity: The Story of Dietrich Bonhoeffer". Uhrichville, OH: Barbour Publishing, Inc, 2001.

Also Available

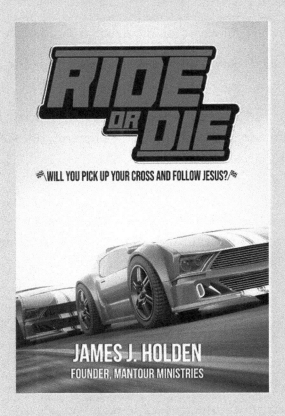

10 Men, One Mission:
To Ride or Die With God!

For more information, visit:
www.mantourministries.com/rideordie

ALSO AVAILABLE FROM MANTOUR MINISTRIES

Burning Daylight

The Godly Man's Call To Rise and Shine

Whatever It Takes

Living A Life Worthy Of Your Calling

Under Construction

We're All Men Under Construction!

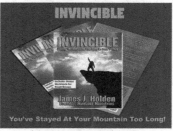

INVINCIBLE

You've Stayed At Your Mountain Too Long!

Get In The Game

It's Time To Get Out Of The Locker Room and Get In The Game!

Legacy: Living A Life That Lasts

How Will You Be Remembered?

PUTTING ON MANHOOD

IT'S TIME TO PUT ON GODLY MANHOOD!

Available in print and digital formats. Visit www.mantourministries.com for more information.

I'd love to come share a challenging word of victory!

CONTACT ME TO COME SHARE.

DEFEAT IS NOT AN OPTION!

Jamie loves to speak to men and is available to speak at your next men's event. Jamie combines humor and his personal testimony to both engage and challenge men to grow in their walk with God. He uses his testimony of overcoming abuse as well as dealing with his physical and emotional issues growing up to encourage men that no matter what their background or where they have come from in life, they can grow into mighty men in God's kingdom.

"Years ago, while I was attending the University of Valley Forge, God gave me a deep desire to minister to men. My calling is to help men learn what it means to be a godly man and how to develop a deep, personal relationship with their heavenly Father. We strive to challenge and encourage men to reach their full potential in God's kingdom."

If you are interested in having Jamie at your next men's event as a speaker or workshop leader, or if you are interested in having him come share with your church, e-mail him at jamie@mantourministries.com. He is also available to speak for one or multiple weeks on the theme of his books, Burning Daylight, Whatever It Takes, Invincible: Scaling The Mountains That Keep Us From Victory. Putting On Manhood, Legacy: Living a Life that Lasts, and Get in the Game.